INFLATION
IN THE
CARIBBEAN

Edited by
COMPTON BOURNE

INSTITUTE OF SOCIAL AND ECONOMIC RESEARCH
UNIVERSITY OF THE WEST INDIES
MONA, JAMAICA
1977

First published 1977
by Institute of Social and Economic Research
University of the West Indies, Mona, Kingston 7, Jamaica.

© 1977, Institute of Social and Economic Research

This is the fifth of a series of studies that have been undertaken under the programme of Regional Monetary Studies. This programme has been financed by the Central Banks of the Bahamas, Barbados, Guyana, Jamaica and Trinidad and Tobago, the Eastern Caribbean Currency Authority and the Monetary Authority of Belize. The programme is being undertaken on a collaborative basis by the Institute of Social and Economic Research, University of the West Indies and the Department of Economics, University of Guyana and is designed to carry out a wide variety of investigations on monetary and financial matters in the region.

In the best academic tradition, our sponsors, while participating in decisions about the planning of the programme, have not attempted to influence the conduct of the research or the conclusions drawn, which are those of the authors alone.

CONTENTS

ACKNOWLEDGEMENTS

The papers contained in this volume are a selection from the Seventh Annual Conference of the Regional Programme of Monetary Studies held in Georgetown, Guyana 13–15 October, 1975.

The Regional Programme of Monetary Studies on behalf of all the participants would like to record its sincere appreciation of the facilities graciously provided by its host, the Bank of Guyana.

A debt is owed to the staff of the Bank, especially Mr. Aggrey King, and Miss Nola Sinclair as well as to staff of the University of Guyana for their generous devotion of time and energy without which the Conference could not have been the pleasant and productive occasion it undoubtedly was.

COMPTON BOURNE

INTRODUCTION

Research into inflation in the Commonwealth Caribbean has been quite spasmodic, with each wave of studies coinciding with a marked upward movement in the rate of price increases from what has been a basically mild inflationary situation for these economies.

The initial inflationary studies were those of Brewster [2,3] and Hall [4] though inflation strictly defined was not the centre of their interest. The central concern of both writers was wage-productivity relationships and the then topical issue of wage policy as a means of securing comparative advantage in international trade. Nonetheless, both studies appeared about 1967 when the sympathetic devaluation of Caribbean currencies with the pound sterling resulted in a marked increase in the general level of prices.

The 1972 and 1973 devaluations served as the stimuli for the second wave of studies. As the titles of the papers by Joefield-Napier [5] Latibeaudiere [6] Ramjeesingh [7] and St. Cyr [8] indicate, the focus of interest on this occasion was inflation, largely from the perspective of diagnosis. These authors adduced with differing degrees of statistical support and rigour, explanations in terms of wage push, economic openness measured by foreign-trade-GNP ratios, import prices, deficit financing and some other demand-pull factors, and markups in the distribution sector.

The papers in this volume constitute the main results of the third wave of studies. The stimulus to research was yet another upward displacement of the rate of price increases in 1974. On this occasion, however, inflation assumed unaccustomed proportions of 20 to 38 per cent in some countries. As on previous occasions, domestic inflation appeared to be externally induced – the massive rise in oil prices and the continuing depreciation of the pound sterling serving as the main villains of the piece. Unlike in the earlier inflationary periods, domestic factors, notably deficit financing and supply deficiencies, also seemed *a priori* to be important inflationary impulses. Moreover, the sheer proportion of the inflation and its implications for political and social performance imparted an unprecedented degree of urgency to the search for appropriate anti-inflation policies.

The latter consideration made for an important difference between earlier studies and the ones included in this volume. The current set of studies is the outgrowth of a systematic review and exploration of the contemporary Caribbean inflation in a framework that sought to guide policy. The Seventh Annual Conference of the Regional Programme of Monetary Studies at which the papers were presented was comprised of central bankers and academic researchers coming together for sustained, open discussion of the inflation problem.

The rest of this introduction gives a guided tour of the main contents of the volume, discusses the main findings in relation to earlier results, points out the continuing relevance of the study and of anti-inflationary policy prescriptions, and finally outlines some policy guidelines.

All the papers review in differing detail the course of inflation in the Associated States, the Bahamas, Barbados, Guyana, Jamaica, Trinidad and Tobago, and Latin America during the 1970s. The historical review of price trends is the main objective of the papers by Whittingham, William Allen, Francis, and Joefield-Napier. Three papers — Bourne and Persaud, Manhertz, Joefield-Napier — model various aspects of the inflationary process. Manhertz utilising annual data focuses on the role of cost variables. Joefield-Napier uses the Cagan technique to analyse the formation of price expectations. In addition, he examines by regression methods the impact of inflation on the income velocity of money over the period 1959-1972. Bourne and Persaud focus on the short period influence of selected financial variables, notably money supply, bank rate and exchange rates on the pace of inflation within the framework of a structural model. Errol Allen and Gloria Francis attempt non-econometric empirical explanations of inflation in the Associated States and in Barbados respectively. One paper (by Jefferson and Boyce) assesses the effects of foreign and domestic inflation on a sample of Caribbean economies consisting of a more developed economy (Jamaica), an intermediate economy (Barbados), and on a Caribbean lesser developed economy (Dominica). The final paper by Jack Guenther describes and appraises the system of indexation adopted in Brazil since 1964.

The studies contained in this volume generate a series of results, some less tentative than other, which serve to reinforce and sometimes give more rigorous validity to earlier hypothesis. In general they advance our knowledge of the causes and effects of inflation in the Caribbean. The main findings will now be identified.

Import prices are shown to be the main inflationary stimuli. Brewster [2,3] in his earlier works had noted that increases in import prices paralleled increases in domestic retail prices in Jamaica and Guyana. From this he inferred that import prices were a push element in Caribbean inflation. St. Cyr [8], utilising annual data in a regression study of Trinidad and Tobago for the period 1951 to 1972, established that "domestic prices have been pushed up by import prices principally". These results are confirmed for different time periods and with different methods by several papers in this volume. Thus Bourne-Persaud and Manhertz in econometric studies with quarterly data and annual data for Jamaica conclude that the major generating factor is import prices. Bourne-Persaud also arrive at the same conclusion for Trinidad and Tobago, as on the basis of tabular analyses do William Allen for the Bahamas, Errol Allen for Montserrat and St. Kitts, and Gloria Francis for Barbados.

In all cases, the degree of imported inflation is directly related to the degree of import-dependence and openness of the economies. Though Caribbean economies are not exactly homogeneous with respect to the degree of openness they are all highly import-dependent, whether one is dealing with for example, Jamaica with an import-GNP ratio of 40 per cent or with the Bahamas with an import-GNP ratio of 60 per cent. Despite so many years of import-substituting industrialisation and partly because of a failure to develop agriculture for the domestic market, Caribbean economies are still very vulnerable to external price behaviour. Whittingham shows that Latin America is not much better off in this respect.

Import prices are a linear combination of foreign import prices (inclusive of freight and insurance) and domestic exchange rate changes. While in fixed exchange rate regimes one can ignore the latter element, it is obvious that under a regime of variable exchange rates this source of price determination cannot be ignored. Exchange rate changes become a means of stabilising or destabilising the domestic price level. Trinidad and Tobago, and tne Associated States because of their link with the pound sterling experienced continued fluctuations in their exchange rates from 1972, thereby providing data for testing the influence of exchange rate movements on domestic price behaviour. Bourne and Persaud undertook such a study for Trinidad and Tobago. They regressed the logarithm of import prices on the logarithms ot the export prices of Trinidad and Tobago's trading partners and of the exchange rate for the first quarter 1971 to fourth quarter 1974. The result establishes that exchange rate changes contributed significantly to changes in import prices (explaining roughly 27 per cent of the changes in import prices). The second main finding of the study, therefore, is that exchange rate depreciation has had an important effect on the pace of inflation in Trinidad and Tobago, and by logical extension possibly in the Associated States.

All the studies reported in the volume conclude that despite the predominant influence of import prices, the nature and pace of inflation in the Caribbean cannot be explained entirely by external factors. Caribbean inflation in the 1970s is to some extent endogenously determined, and to a much greater degree than recognised by earlier writers, notably Brewster [2,3]. There is no unanimity, however, among the authors as to the relative importance of various domestic explanatory variables.

Wage rate changes as a cost-push factor are dealt with by Bourne and Persaud, by Manhertz, and by Errol Allen. Bourne and Persaud conclude that statistically wage rate changes are important in the explanation of inflation in Trinidad and Tobago — a result which is consistent with St. Cyr's findings on the basis of annual data. On the other hand, Manhertz's regression of prices on wage/income ratios for Jamaica yielded a negative relationship thereby contradicting the wage-push hypothesis. Errol Allen argues against wage push on the basis of impressionistic evidence. He argues that trade union militancy is tempered by the close linkage between the major trade union and the governing party, by the large share of peasant production in economic activity and by the unions' acceptance of the fact that profitability in export industries, their major source of employment, is externally determined.

The wage-price relationship evokes much controversy in the Caribbean and elsewhere perhaps largely because of its political implications. Some points of debate are easily dispensed with. For instance, the common misconception that evidence of money wages lagging behind price increases disproves the existence of wage-push inflation. Clearly this is so if one is dealing with original causes — but in a dynamic situation such causes can hardly ever be pinpointed. Moreover, an inflationary situation is by nature dynamic. In such contexts, the wage price relationship is best seen as an element in a social or class struggle — one in which attempts of workers to maintain or to increase real wages are resisted by employers with consequent upward pressures on prices. If workers keep losing that struggle, as they have done for reasons hypothesized by Bourne [1], then real wages would lag behind prices, but a round of wage increases would have initiated a round of price increases. In other words, there would have been an element of wage-push inflation.

Any clear understanding of the role of wages in the inflationary mechanism must await the results of detailed studies of many features of the labour market. Among these must be the nature and empirical significance of labour militancy, the effects of wages and incomes policy on wage settlements, bargaining strategies and outcomes, the bases of producer resistance and producer power, and the influence of prices in wage-demand functions. The last-mentioned has particular significance for the self-generating character of inflation — lagged prices pushing current wages, and current wages then pushing future prices. Bourne and Persaud have established a weak statistical relationship between changes in the current wage rate and changes in prices lagged up to four quarters. Their result is however far from definitive.

There is yet another feature of inflationary dynamics on which the volume sheds some light. Recent models of inflation pay much attention to price expectations. In particular it is recognised that price expectations can be de-stabilising if people react to anticipations of higher future rates of price increases by accelerating their current period expenditures thereby exaggerating excess demand pressures in the current period. On the other hand, static expectations are not destabilising. It is therefore important, to establish quantitatively the process of price expectation formation. Joefield-Napier in his study has done so for Jamaica. He concludes that price expectations are revised very slowly, the length of the lag being about four years. As a result "price expectations effects did not have an instantaneous impact upon domestic price formation, but filtered ..... through the economy". [Napier p. 28]. It is useful to note that Napier discovered that expected prices generally exceeded actual prices, which implies a somewhat pessimistic community.

The roles of monetary and credit variables were explored by Joefield-Napier and Bourne and Persaud, as well as by the two Allens and by Whittingham. Only the study by Whittingham supports a propulsive role for monetary expansion. Bourne and Persaud conclude that in Trinidad and Tobago, the gross deficit of the central government exerted a depressing effect on price movements, while for both Trinidad and Tobago as well as for Jamaica the commercial bank prime loan rate is a push-factor in domestic inflation. It is noteworthy that Joefield-Napier finds that in Jamaica money demand is inelastic with respect to price expectations when money is narrowly defined, but not when money is more broadly defined. His findings indicate that price expectations do not augment expenditure functions.

Errol Allen advanced the potentially important hypothesis that inflation might have been transmitted from the more developed Caribbean countries to the lesser developed ones. Though he has not provided any evidence in support of his hypothesis, it is easy to accept it on *a priori* grounds. The theoretical basis is essentially the open economy postulate regionalised to the Caribbean. With the development of intra-Caribbean trade and in particular with the growing share of the exports from Trinidad and Tobago and Barbados in LDC imports, there is a shift in the locus of trade dependence. With this shift comes the possibility of the regional transmission of inflation provided that inflation rates in the Caribbean MDCs exceed those in the LDCs. This condition was satisfied during the first half of the 1970s.

Turning now to the effects of inflation, one can list a few findings of the wide-ranging paper by Jefferson and Boyce. They conclude *inter alia* that (i) the ability of Caribbean countries to finance the increasing value of imported producer goods was substantially increased as a result of inflationary conditions in their export markets; (ii) there was a shift in the structure of imports away from consumer goods; (iii) the structure of consumption altered in favour of domestically produced commodities; (iv) government expenditures and hence employment growth were restrained; (v) downturns resulted in tourism, construction and manufacturing, and (vi) a redistribution of income towards property-owners and the stronger sections of unionised workers. In short, inflation had a generally adverse effect on Caribbean economies.

During 1976 Caricom economies had some respite from the high rates of inflation experienced during 1974 and 1975. There was a decline in the rate of increases in the general level of retail prices though by different degrees in the several economies. While in 1975, the rate of inflation ranged from 6.7 per cent to 20.3 per cent, in 1976 the range was 3.7 per cent to 12.4 per cent.

Nonetheless a few important observations indicate that there is still little basis for comfort, and correspondingly that these studies are of continuing relevance. Firstly, the rates of inflation are too high in relation to productivity, especially in the export industries, in relation to increases in labour incomes, and in relation to the growth in government budgets especially in the lesser developed countries. As a consequence, the current rates of inflation still exert a serious adverse influence on export performance, on domestic living standards, and on the real financial capacities of the governments.

Secondly, the areas with the largest price increases have been the main basic types of consumer expenditures. The expenditure groups for which price increases were greater than 10 per cent in 1976 vary across countries. Generally speaking, they include food, transportation, clothing, fuel, electricity, water, education, medical expenses and housing and house furnishing. The fact that the burden of price increases is concentrated in these areas of social concern underscores the conclusion that inflation is an important problem and should rank high on the policy agenda.

Thirdly, the social incidence of Caribbean inflation is also of critical importance to trade union wage demands and to the scope for successful wage restraint policies. The lessons of international experience with incomes policies are abundantly clear on this point. Wages policies cannot work when the living standards of workers are seriously eroded by rising prices. Nor can worker morale and productivity be reasonably expected to be high under such conditions.

Fourthly, the persistence of relatively high rates of inflation in Trinidad and Tobago and in Barbados is not solely a national issue, but becomes one for regional concern. The regional transmission of inflation affects living standards, exports via the costs of production, and budgets among other things in the lesser developed countries. It also imposes strains on Caricom trade at times when rates of inflation in the more developed countries exceed the rate of increase in export prices from the metropolitan trading partners of the lesser developed countries.

The results of the studies in this volume as well as the earlier studies indicate that to constrain the rate of price increases within tolerable limits, anti-inflation policy has to be broadly based. In the package of measures or the armoury as Whittingham terms it, must be prices and income restraint policies. By a careful policy of price control, not only can price increases in some key commodity markets be moderated, but the spread effects can also be reduced in so far as workers react to increases in the prices of the main household budget items. Given the cost-plus basis of pricing and the tendency for cost increases to originate externally, a rational price restraint policy has to be based on the conscious policy decision that profits must be squeezed. The business community must accept part of the burden of adjustment to adverse international conditions. It is worth noting that under the inflationary conditions which prevailed in the first half of the 1970s, the share of profits in national income grew.

Incomes policies have so far been at best partial in their scope, amounting to restraints on wage rates and on public sector salaries. The omission of private sector salaries especially at the upper end of the income scale, is particularly significant in the more developed countries such as Jamaica and Trinidad and Tobago where there is a large private sector. One undesirable but inexorable consequence of incomes restraint policies has been a further deterioration in the distribution of personal incomes. As a result, not only are social tensions exacerbated, but the resistance of the masses to wage policies hardens. The recognition of these facts underlies current attempts at developing a broadly based incomes policy in Jamaica.

Apart from its intrinsic merit on social and labour productivity grounds, a basic needs consumption policy should constitute an additional critical element in the battle against inflation. In this context, its rationale is its role as an inducement for workers' co-operation with wages and incomes guidelines. The provision for basic needs is at one and the same time an assurance that living standards will not be eroded beyond socially tolerable limits by inflation under conditions of wage and income restraints.

However, it is self-evident, given the balance of payments constraint, that a basic needs policy is not remotely realisable without substantial increases in domestic production. Output also needs to be expanded to close the excess demand gap. Another important solution to excess demand problems is Caricom trade in consumer goods, inclusive of food, under credit arrangements.

A variety of balance of payments support measures can also be adopted. These could include —

(a) credit arrangements on Caricom trade;
(b) subsidised sales of essential goods, e.g. oil and other petroleum products to Caricom partners; and
(c) general credit facilities.

The first and third measures would enable a higher level of imports to augment domestic supplies and thereby moderate excess demand pressures. In both cases, credit could be extended on a Central Bank to Central Bank basis. In the first case, the Central Bank in the exporting country would pay the private exporter and in turn accept the liabilities of the importing country's Central Bank. The second measure would serve to reduce input prices and thereby moderate cost push inflationary tendencies.

Another potentially useful set of anti-inflationary measures is state importation and distribution. State importation would facilitate bulk purchases and the establishment of cheaper sources of credit, particularly in non-traditional markets thereby providing a basis for slowing down increases in the prices of basic inputs and final goods. Caribbean governments could collaborate in bulk purchases in the search for cheaper sources, and in the exchange of trading information, so that the best possible deals are available to each and all of them. State distribution may well turn out to be one of the most important planks in the basic needs policy. At the very minimum, it would help to alleviate shortages, especially those contrived as a means of pressuring governments to award price increases on strategic consumer goods.

At a more conventional level there needs to be some restraint on government consumption expenditures, the stabilisation of exchange rates, and the adoption of low interest rate policies which would serve to reduce cost push pressures.

To be sure, not all the findings nor policy conclusions embodied in this volume would command the support of all economists and policymakers. However if the studies do no more than provoke further research on the continuing problem of inflation in the Caribbean, their publication 'would have served a useful purpose.

REFERENCES

[1] Bourne, Compton, "Structure, Power and Wage-Price Policy in the West Indies", *Journal of Social and Behavioural Sciences*, Vol. 20, No. 4, 1974.

[2] Brewster, Havelock, "Wage, Price and Productivity Relations in Jamaica, 1957 to 1962", *Social and Economic Studies*, Vol. 17, No. 2, 1968.

[3] ——————— "The Pattern of Changes in Wages, Prices and Productivity in British Guiana, 1948 to 1962", *Social and Economic Studies*, Vol. 18, No. 2, 1969.

[4] Hall, Marshall, "An Analysis of the Determinants of Money Wage Changes in Jamaica 1958–64", *Social and Economic Studies*, Vol. 17, No. 2, 1968.

[5] Joefield-Napier, Wallace, "Jamaican Inflation 1959–1972", ISER, UWI, Mimeo 1974.

[6] Latibeaudiere, D.M., "An Analysis of Inflation in Jamaica", Bank of Jamaica Mimeo, September 1974.

[7] Ramjeesingh, D.H., "Inflation in Trinidad and Tobago", Department of Economics, UWI, Mimeo 1974.

[8] St. Cyr, E.B.A., "Rising Prices: An Explanatory Theoretical and Empirical Study of Trinidad and Tobago", *Central Statistical Office Research Papers*, No. 7, 1974.

HUNTLEY G. MANHERTZ

THE PRICE DETERMINATION PROCESS IN A SMALL OPEN ECONOMY — THE JAMAICAN EXPERIENCE

INTRODUCTION [1]

This investigation has as its main focus the examination and explanation of the movements of retail or consumer prices in Jamaica. By necessity, there is also some examination of those economic factors which influence the overall behaviour of domestic prices at the different levels of major economic activity (i.e., production, distribution and consumption). Although the character and overall economic effect of the price causation mechanism are discussed, the analysis should by no means be considered exhaustive in respect of the Jamaican economy.

Some of the more interesting and important problems to which this investigation is directed are as follows: (1) the isolation of those economic variables which significantly influence domestic price levels and the changes in these levels over time. The primary consideration is with price movements rather than price levels. (2) The nature and the degree of the movement of prices. An examination of the rate of price increase as it relates to the levels of domestic productivity should provide a satisfactory basis to verify the existence and degree of inflation. (3) The extent to which economic growth and economic stability are influenced by the interacting forces of aggregate output levels, productivity, and the movement in price levels. (4) The policy rationale for a continuous adjustment of the price formation mechanism in order to arrive at, and maintain, some desirable optimum for purposes of economic stability, while simultaneously facilitating a desired rate of growth.

Generally, in the study of price determination and price movements, essentially two basic types of approaches may be used. The analysis may focus exclusively on market prices (i.e. prices which are involved in exchange at the market level). These market or exchange prices may be initially determined within the general framework of at least three basic theoretical propositions, these are marginal cost; target return; and mark-up pricing. The analysis of market prices obviously provides the option of investigating either wholesale prices (at the primary level of trade transaction) or retail prices. However, the degree of variability and statistical intractability which is usually characteristic of retail prices in a free market situation, quite often render wholesale prices more amenable to analysis.

The second type of approach which may be used is what may be called the 'value-added' model. This framework is based on value-added price or the price at the producer level. Value-added price should really be interpreted as the value added per unit of output of the commodity and as such excludes the cost of raw materials, and that of intermediate inputs which originate from another source. A formula which is often found to be empirically satisfactory for the estimation of value-added price is as follows:-

$$V_{pi} = \frac{G_{ni}}{G_{oi} - P_{ji}} \; ;$$

where

V_{pi} = value-added price in the i th industry

G_{ni} = gross product originating in industry i at current prices.

G_{oi} = gross output of industry i at constant prices

P_{ji} = purchases of industry i from industry j at constant prices.

From the above algebraic expression, it is clear that the quantity $(G_{oi} - P_{ji})$ represents value-added in constant dollars. In fact the value-added price V_{pi} may be interpreted as the sum of gross factor cost per unit of output for the i th industry.

In the construction of any model on the price formation process, one is therefore always faced with the alternatives of using either market prices or value-added prices. The former represent the basis of management activity and consumer decision-making in respect to final output for any industry, while the latter influence factor use and consequently, the form of the production function for an industry. It must, however, be pointed out that in the case of Jamaica, adequate data have not been assembled on wholesale prices nor on value-added prices. Any meaningful investigation of price formation which utilises secondary statistical data must therefore be confined to the use of retail prices.[2]

AN OVERVIEW OF THE THEORY OF PRICE DETERMINATION

The price formation process for a firm, an industry, or in any market, may either be conveniently explained in terms of the perfectly competitive conditions of classical general equilibrium theory, or in terms of the usual deviations from this particular body of theory. Classical theory is essentially idealistic, having as its foundation such assumptions as perfect knowledge about all factors affecting the market, non-differentiability of commodities, absolute non-rigidity in the mobility of factor inputs, and some upper limit to individual market share. The deviations from these conditions of absolute perfection in the market-place are usually described in terms of an entire range of possible buyer-seller relationships, and go from the case of the one seller-many buyers interaction (monopoly) to that of the one buyer-many sellers interaction (monopsony). Modern markets, however, for the most part operate on the basis of these so-called imperfections as suggested by Richardson [17] and others, and more recently empirically observed by Lanzioletti [13].

Classical equilibrium theory provides the foundation for that analysis of price formation which is based on marginal analysis, and which is often referred to as marginal cost pricing. The basic guideline behind the concept of marginal cost pricing is that at all times the market conditions can only be considered favourable to any firm if each incremental return (marginal revenue) is equal to each incremental outlay (marginal cost). This approach to the explanation of the price formation process is also in itself very idealistic.

In most industries, and for most firms, the pricing principle which is used is one which is geared to ensure a minimum rate of return to capital outlay. This approach to pricing is called target return pricing. It has as a special derivative an approach which de-emphasizes the optimality conditions which are normally required for a prescribed target rate of return, and simply incorporates an assessed mark-up over average cost. In the case of target-return pricing, the equilibrium price for market clearing is directly determined by the factor shares from the production function.[3] Mark-up pricing, because of its implicit arbitrary nature, often appears to be a relatively unsophisticated approach to pricing. This technique, however, represents one which is quite widely used, particularly among smaller firms operating in a less than perfectly competitive market. Since mark-up pricing is simply a special form of target-return pricing, it would be safe to say that for most market economies the principle of target-return pricing is fundamental to the price formation process. It therefore follows that the structure of the price formation process in most market economies represents a deviation from conditions of perfect competition.

Irrespective of the type of price determination mechanism being studied, the general character of the cost function is of paramount importance. In the case of the target-return and mark-up models, however, the structure of cost is taken as given, then adjustments are made in the form of a mark-up over cost in order to generate a satisfactory surplus level of revenues. In general, any price determination mechanism for Jamaica should be investigated in terms of stocks and flows (i.e. inventory levels and market disequilibrium) as well as in terms of short-run cost factors such as labour, material and, in the case of imports, the unit value or c.i.f. (cost, insurance and freight) price.[4]

The present model will therefore incorporate both the stock-flow and mark-up hypotheses. The empirical character of both hypotheses as is manifested for the Jamaican economy will be examined together and not individually. In fact, to the extent that the magnitude of the mark-up over unit cost may directly influence the demand for a good, and consequently the equilibrium market conditions, there exists a demonstrable theoretical relation between the mark-up and stock flow models.[5]

ANALYTICAL FRAMEWORK

As was earlier suggested, because of the non-availability of adequate information on prices at the primary levels of economic activity (i.e. production and wholesale distribution) the empirical portrayal and analysis of price formation for the Jamaican economy will be necessarily confined to the retail market.

The assessment and explanation of the movements of market prices are usually made on the basis of appropriately weighted aggregative indices of the prices of select goods and services (a market basket) in reference to an 'ideal' base period. In the case of retail prices, the underlying sampling design entails not only the representative sampling of the relevant goods and services, but also the consumer units by income levels and geographic location. This index of retail or consumer prices has been traditionally the most popularly used yardstick in measuring changes in the purchasing power in an economy over time.

Despite the apparent usefulness and versatility of the index of consumer prices, it could however be argued that this index represents an aggregative measurement of prices at the final stage of the distribution process (the retail stage) and may not necessarily reflect the character of price changes earlier in the line of economic activity. This deficiency is also quite likely to exist at sectoral and industry levels (i.e. manufacturing, construction, etc.). The incapacity to adequately reflect quality changes from the base period also represents an important limitation in the use of any index number as a measuring tool. The above limitations are common to all indices of retail prices, and although these indices provide a satisfactory measure of price change, it is of paramount importance that their interpretation should be guided by those inherent limitations.[6]

As far as Jamaica is concerned, there are two important considerations which serve to aggravate the limitations which have already been suggested. The first has to do with the fact that at the time this study was undertaken, there did not exist a single index to measure island-wide price changes. Up through December of 1974, two separate indices were used, one for the Kingston metropolitan area and the other for the rest of the island. The latter is what is called the index of rural retail prices. The analysis in this paper is based on that particular set of data.[7]

The second important limiting consideration in regard to the index of retail prices in Jamaica, and particularly to the series upon which the analysis is based, is the composition (with respect to content) of the non-durable categories in the 'market basket', particularly as this relates to the efficiency of the index in measuring changes in the purchasing power of middle and upper income consumers. Many items such as charcoal, poultry feed, and others, which were frequently consumed in the average Jamaican household of the 1950s are not now widely consumed. Noticeably absent from the category of durables are such common household appliances as refrigerators, cooking stoves and household gadgets. It should be emphasised that the usefulness of any index of consumer prices is almost totally determined by the relevance or timeliness of the goods and services constituting the 'market basket'.

For purposes of this study, the hypothetical or philosophical view behind retail price movements in Jamaica, will be presented in terms of three broad categories; the influences of cost (actual and normal) and output variations on the supply side, the effect of *ad hoc* mark-up, and the positive psychological motivation of consumers which combines with other non-market forces to directly or indirectly influence decision-making in the market place. Those factors which make up the third category are not usually amenable to direct quantification. It would therefore be anticipated that cost and supply variations represent the major factors on which the price formation process may be satisfactorily explained.[8]

Cost

The general effect of cost on the behaviour of prices may be viewed in terms of the relationship between the normal operating cost of the firm and short-run deviations from this norm. That level of cost which results as a consequence of short-run deviations from normal operating cost may be considered to be the actual current cost of operation. Normal cost then may be taken to represent the long-run average cost which prevails for the firm or industry. Some factors such as labour supply and utilisation, level of productivity, raw material availability, and unplanned inventory change, usually exhibit a relatively high degree of fluctuation for certain industries, and these short-run changes are usually expected to be mirrored by the general movement of prices.[9] There is, however, a strong tendency for an immediate upward adjustment in prices in cases of a negative fluctuation (i.e. a downward movement) of any of those factors. On the other hand, the effect of a positive fluctuation, which should normally give rise to a price decrease, is either lagged over an appreciable time period or is totally non-effective. This peculiar relationship between the movement of actual cost and the adjustment of prices produces a typical 'ratchet' or irreversibility effect, and is quite common in those markets where the mark-up principle is used in pricing.[10] Since the fluctuations are in fact essentially short-run in character, the existence of the 'ratchet effect' invariably produces increased profit levels after a return to the normal levels of operation. This represents one explanation of the profit-price spiral recently experienced by many firms (particularly manufacturing and distributing).

On the whole, however, the use of cost as a satisfactory explanatory factor in the analysis of the price formation process in Jamaica is expected to present two important problems. First, the quality of the data (current and historical) which are available on actual cost is very poor for most Jamaican firms. This is particularly evident at the level of commodity aggregation which is used in this analysis. Attempts were made to empirically measure the effect of prime cost in terms of the current rate of interest (commercial lending rate), an index of import (c.i.f.) prices, and net indirect taxes per dollar of consumption expenditure. As will be demonstrated later, only the effect of import prices is recognizable to any appreciable degree at the retail level.

The second major problem which will be encountered in respect to the explanatory capacity of cost in studying price formation in Jamaica is the difficulty of estimating normal cost for a firm or industry. The use of negotiated unit factor payments such as the average wage rate, represents an appropriate approach to assessing normal cost, but in the case of Jamaica, there are no assembled data on such payments by firms or industries. A reasonable compromise in the case of this study, will be the ratio of wages to actual output by commodity groups or industries, whichever is more feasible.[11] This ratio of the wage bill to gross output by industry groups (sectors) is assumed to approximate the long-run average unit labour cost which influences the movement of the average price for each commodity group. As will be observed later, the index of this cost does not reflect any significant effect on price change for most commodity groups. In most cases, there is an inverse relationship which suggests that long-run average cost has decreased over the sample period and therefore other factors have served more to appreciably influence price change.

Supply Variations

It was earlier suggested that in addition to cost, there is also the effect of variations in supply, reflected in the movement of domestic prices. In this respect, the actual value of physical inventory change will be incorporated for purposes of assessing the effect of demand pressure for a given commodity group. This demand pressure (or excess demand) is in fact a consequence of market disequilibrium. The effect of output variation should normally be measured in terms of gross product per man, or per hour. The availability of these data on an industry basis is however quite limited, and a suitable proxy will therefore have to be an index of real value produce originating at the industry level.

Non-market Factors

With regard to the so-called non-market factors to which earlier reference was made, some of these factors are either directly non-quantifiable as would be the case of consumer panic buying (irrespective of price) when shortages are anticipated or may be indirectly reflected by some primary explanatory factors. An example of the latter would be the case of increased levels of *ad hoc* markups in cases of a positive deviation of actual from normal cost.[12] The profit rate (i.e. the ratio of profit to gross product) does not always move in one-to-one relation with average cost and the level of output. The variable is, however, of much importance particularly in respect of understanding the anticipatory element in price formation. There is an inadequacy of statistical information on industry profits to make possible a satisfactory evaluation of this variable.

Generally, a comprehensive assessment of price determination should be made within a simultaneous equation framework in view of the joint endogenous character of such key explanatory factors as wages, output, inventory demand, and so on. This investigation will, however, de-emphasize the statistical merits of simultaneity in so far as an overall examination of the selected explanatory factors is concerned. The empirical model will therefore consist essentially of a series of single-equation estimates of the price function for particular commodity groupings. Since each commodity group and sub-group, can be assumed to be relatively homogeneous in respect to the price formation processes earlier discussed, there will be as many market structures *per se* as there are commodity groups. The effect of the respective explanatory factors could therefore be considered unique with respect to a particular commodity group. This would suggest a condition of exogeneity characterising the selected explanatory factors, and would therefore serve to ensure that the estimates generated are of acceptable statistical quality.

THE DATA

As has already been pointed out, this exercise involves the explanation of the movement of consumer or retail prices in a small open economy and an empirical evaluation of the situation in respect to the Jamaican economy. To accomplish this, a number of commodity groups have been isolated, and the movement of these prices will be explained in terms of select explanatory variables which are assumed to be essentially pre-determined as far as the price formation process is concerned. The set of explanatory factors for each commodity group is individually defined for the Kingston and Rural areas. The following item categories and sub-categories will be individually examined.[13]

1. All items in the Market Basket for the Consumer Price Index (A)
2. Food and Drink (D)
   a) Fresh Meat and Fish (D^{mf})
   b) Tinned and Pickled Meat and Fish (D^{mp})
   c) Starchy Roots and Vegetables (D^{rv})
   d) Starchy Fruits (D^{fs})
   e) Other Fruits and Vegetables (D^{fo})
   f) Bread, Cereal, and Sugar (D^{bc})
   g) Dairy Products, Fats and Oils (D^{do})
   h) Beverages and Other Food Items (D^{bo})
3. Fuel and Cleaning (F)
4. Rent and Fixed Household Costs (R)
   a) Rent (R^{rt})

b) Other Household Cost	(R^{ok})
5. Personal Expenses	(P)
a) Medical Expenses	(p^{md})
b) Other Personal Expenses	(p^{oe})
6. Clothing	(C)
a) Material	(C^{ma})
b) Making-up	(C^{kp})
c) Household Linen	(C^{w})
d) Footwear	(C^{ft})
e) Other Clothing (socks, stockings, headgear, etc.)	(C^{og})
7. Household Expenses	(H)
a) Transportation	(H^{tr})
b) Education	(H^{ed})
c) Insurance	(H^{in})
d) Durables (Equipment and Furniture)	(H^{du})
e) Other Household Expenses (wages, etc.)	(H^{ox})

In most cases, however, the nature of the price formation process for these sub-categories was statistically non-recognizable from the available sample data, and the analysis therefore has to be undertaken on a less rigorous basis. The major explanatory variables which were found to be empirically relevant for the respective categories and sub-categories over the sample period are symbolized as follows:-

w/y	=	ratio of industry wage-bill to gross product originating
p^m	=	index of c.i.f. prices
p^{mf}	=	index of c.i.f. prices for food
v/y	=	ratio of inventory change to gross product originating

The available data on the index of retail prices exist in two forms which cannot be easily merged. The first complete series of price indices was generated from a 'market basket' assembled in 1955 and has as base the retail prices for January 1955. This series extends through 1966, and as of 1967 a new series was developed. The latter series has as base January 1967, and there was an appreciable increase in the content of the 'market basket'. This increase was necessary because of changes in consumption patterns for the respective commodity groups over time. Such changes invariably involve the inclusion of new items which heretofore were not widely consumed (e.g. ready-made clothing) or the exclusion of items the consumption of which has decreased appreciably by volume (e.g. twisted tobacco). As earlier pointed out, a new series with Janaury 1975 as its reference period has been developed.

EMPIRICAL RESULTS[14]

This study examines the behaviour of consumer prices over the period 1956 through the final quarter of 1974. In some cases, it has been possible to isolate and explain the effects of some primary causative factors which have influenced the movements in these prices, particularly for the 1957-1966 time period. An explicit illustration of the relationship between price movements and the relevant explanatory variable was limited to this period primarily because of the fact that satisfactory explanatory data were not available for a longer period. The general character of these relationships may however be extrapolated with a satisfactory degree of statistical confidence into that period preceding the sample period as well as later through to the present time.

All Items

A preliminary assessment of the movement in consumer prices should first be made by examining the rate of change in the indices for the two respective periods since 1955 during which, as earlier observed, there are some change in the calculation of the index itself. As can be seen from Table 1 between the first quarter of 1956 and December of 1966, the aggregate index of consumer prices for all items purchased increased by an average rate of about 3.1 per cent per year for the Kingston Area, and of about 2.7 per cent per year for the rural areas. This rate did not only increase for the seven year period (1967-74) which followed, but there was also a shift whereby the increase for the rural areas exceeded that for the Kingston area.

TABLE 1
CONTRASTING AVERAGE ANNUAL RATES OF PRICE INCREASE (PER CENT)

PERIOD	Kingston Area	Rural Areas
January 1956 – December 1966 (January 1955 = 100)	3.1	2.7
January 1967 – December 1974 (January 1967 = 100)	7.6	9.0
January 1972 – December 1974 (January 1967 = 100)	25.0	30.0

During this latter period the average annual rates of increase were 7.6 per cent and 9.0 per cent respectively for Kingston and the rest of the country. When examined alongside the rate of increase in gross money output for the nation as a whole, it is interesting to note that during the first ten-year period there was an average annual growth in output of about 7.0 per cent, and for the 1967-74 period this had increased to about 16.0 per cent, indicating that on the average, price increases have not been excessive for the period being reviewed. The evidence would also support the conclusion that rapidly rising prices have not been a characteristic structural feature of the Jamaican economy during its developmental stages for the past 10-15 years.[15] As will be recognised later, however, the period 1971-74 was one of a very high rate of inflation, an experience which might be attributable to movements in some of the more important explanatory variables in the price formation process. It therefore becomes important to assess the extent to which recent inflationary experience of the Jamaican economy is a manifestation of structural adjustments which are likely to persist for some time.

From a statistical standpoint, it is shown in equations 1.0 and 1.1, that the two principal variables which explain the movement of consumer prices in Jamaica are the movement of import prices, and the proportion of gross product which goes to labour (i.e. the ratio of wages to gross output). The latter represents a surrogate for normal labour cost.

1.0   Kingston: $A = 42.01 - \underset{(-2.19)^*}{50.21} \; w/y + \underset{(10.36)^*}{0.84 p^m}$

$$R^2 = 0.94$$
$$Se = 2.87$$
$$D-W = 2.62$$

1.1   Rural: $A = 22.35 + \underset{(13.34)^*}{0.76 p^m} - \underset{(-1.72)}{42.5 \, w/y}$

$$R^2 = 0.96$$
$$Se = 1.87$$
$$D-W = 2.09$$

Interestingly enough, the wage share does not appear to be of any statistical importance as far as changes in the rural consumer price level is concerned, but it is shown to be of some significance for the Kingston area. The variable is interesting, primarily because of the inverse relationship demonstrated. This relationship should not simply be interpreted as a direct inverse one, in that *ceteris paribus* as unit normal costs increase, one would expect prices to decrease, and vice versa. The movement of labour's share of gross output in the case of the

Jamaican economy has not been historically consistent, and this partly explains the negative sign of the estimated normal cost coefficient. Between 1956 and 1966, the share of output going to wages and salaries decreased slightly, and during most of the 1960s held steadily at about 60.0 per cent. In 1972 and again in 1974, there were slight reductions in this share. In order to assess the full effect of wages and salaries on prices, these movements must however be related to changes in labour productivity. When the ratio of gross output to employment is taken as an index for average productivity, it is found that for the period 1957 to 1973, there has been an average annual increase of about 6.50 per cent per year. During the period 1971-74 the average annual increase has been as high as 23.0 per cent. The available data therefore seem to indicate that on the average, there has been a greater increase in the average output per unit of labour than in labour's share of gross output, and therefore labour cost might not have been an important causative factor in increasing price levels for the economy as a whole. It is however likely that this particular variable has been of greater marginal impact in certain industries which by virtue of their relationship with others, as raw material suppliers for example, might have resulted in lagged price increases.[16] Generally, the cost of labour represents an important explanatory variable always to be examined when assessing the structural aspects of the price formation process.

For both geographic areas (Kingston and the rural areas), the effect of import prices on movement in the level of retail prices is quite vivid. Import prices (as shown in equations 1.0 and 1.1) were clearly the most singularly important variables influencing overall price movements in the Jamaican economy for the sample period. When examined by itself, the movement in import prices explains about 92.0 per cent of the variation in retail prices for the Kingston area and about 96.0 per cent for the rural sections of the country.[17]

Essentially, the pattern of movement for import prices is exogenous to the Jamaican economy. These prices are for the most part determined by price levels in the markets from which purchases are made, and are also invariably influenced by changes in the levels of charges for such services as transportation, insurance, and other shipping costs. Table 2 shows a breakdown of visible imports for the years 1955, 1960, 1965, 1970 and 1974 according to the major origins of these imports. The Table also shows the average annual rate of increase of these imports over the same time period.

As can be observed from the Table, the annual rate of increase of imports has been highest for the United States, and for trading partners other than Canada and the United Kingdom. It should however be noted that it has only been since the late 1960s that a drastic shift in the import pattern was realised, particularly as regards both the United States and the category 'rest of the world', as shown in the Table. During the same period under review, export prices of major industrial countries increased only by about 1.8 per cent per year.[18] The real pressure on prices however came on about 1970. For the industrialised countries as a group, these prices increased at a rate of about 7.30 per cent per year between 1968 and 1971, while for most of the 1960s, prior to

TABLE 2   DISTRIBUTION OF VISIBLE IMPORTS BY MAJOR TRADING AREAS

(J$,000)

	1955		1960		1965		1970		1974		AVERAGE ANNUAL GROWTH RATE
	AMT.	PER-CENT	AMT.	PER-CENT	AMT.	PER-CENT	AMT.	PER-CENT	AMT.	PER-CENT	
TOTAL	91,346		155,002		206,470		435,218		850,800		12.50
UNITED STATES	19,032	20.84	37,742	24.35	64,374	31.18	188,400	43.29	399,917	47.00	17.30
UNITED KINGDOM	36,762	40.24	53,256	34.36	50,618	24.52	84,430	19.17	105,325	12.30	5.70
CANADA	10,916	11.95	15,678	10.11	23,258	11.26	39,506	9.08	46,102	5.40	7.80
REST OF WORLD	24,636	26.97	48,326	31.18	68,220	33.04	123,882	28.46	299,456	35.20	14.20

Source: Economic Survey, National Planning Agency

1968, these prices did not change by more than about 1.0 per cent per year. Figure 1 presents the relative movement in the level of export prices which existed in Jamaica's primary supplying markets (the U.S., U.K., and Canada) for the 12-year period 1960-1972 and the contrasting picture presented by movements in the level of our domestic consumer prices (Kingston area) since 1967.[19] The general rapid upward trend of the prices of exports since about 1968 is clearly demonstrated from the graph. The movement in domestic prices has been literally meteoric since 1968, but it is not evident from the data that there has been any obvious generic relationship between the movement of export prices at origin (i.e. for goods imported) and market prices in Jamaica. Though the trend has been generally upwards, the rate of increase in the latter has far outstripped the former with the possible exception of the United Kingdom which has experienced a decreasing share of Jamaica's imports.

When an examination is made of the index of import prices (c.i.f.), it is seen that for the period 1960-1970 (for which fairly accurate up-to-date information is available), these prices increased at an average annual rate of about 2.90 per cent, and for the last three years of that period (1967-1970), the annual rate increased by an average of about 5.6 per cent.

Since 1966, there have been at least five major changes in the foreign exchange position of Jamaica *vis-à-vis* her main trading markets. These changes include the 1967 devaluation of sterling, the devaluation of the United States dollar in 1971 and again in 1973, the 1972 devaluation of the Jamaican dollar and its subsequent realignment in early 1973. Although there is no substantive recognisable empirical evidence, it would seem that during the period 1972-1973, there was some effect of changes in the parity of the Jamaican dollar on price levels. This could have been a consequence of the 1972 Jamaican devaluation. Whereas, there was a 9.4 per cent increase in prices for 1971-72, the 1972-73 increase was in excess of 29.0 per cent. There was a similar experience resulting from the 1967 devaluation of sterling, where the effect on prices during the 1967-68 period was about 5.8 per cent compared with a 2.9 per cent increase in the preceding year.

Although it is clear that there has been some significant effect of changes in import prices on the rate of increase in domestic prices, the fact that there is an appreciable difference in both rates of increase serves to indicate that there are other factors involved in explaining the behaviour of local price levels. Any system of price determination in which the principle of mark-up pricing is widespread, will invariably be subject to the effects of many factors, most of which are nontractable in the statistical sense.[20] It is therefore very likely that an appreciable percentage of price increases is a result of *ad hoc* mark-up in the market. An accurate statistical evaluation of this non-systematic approach to pricing can only be done through an examination of sample survey data on an industry basis, involving all levels of distribution through final consumption.

In an attempt to capture the effect of variations in supply, or conversely the effect of excess demand on changes in retail price levels, the ratio of inventory

FIGURE 1:   RELATIVE MOVEMENTS IN EXPORT PRICES FOR JAMAICA'S MAJOR SUPPLIERS AND IN DOMESTIC RETAIL PRICES

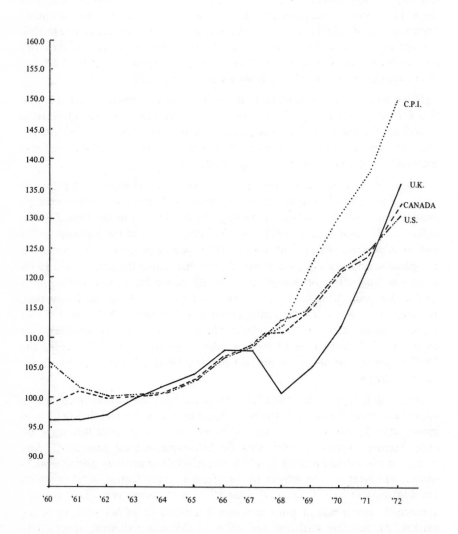

change to gross output for a representative set of commodities was examined. This variable was not shown to be of any relevance for the Kingston area, and for the rural areas could not be considered to be sufficiently statistically significant. The general conclusion would therefore be that for the period, changes in the inventory levels for goods were not sufficiently large to be reflected in changes in retail prices. It should however be borne in mind that changes in aggregate inventory levels may add out, and the major potential effect as regards price movements would therefore be manifested in the physical inventory of individual goods.

Food and Drink

Between 1957 and 1966, the prices of food and drink in the Kingston area increased at an average annual rate of about 2.9 per cent, and for the period 1967-1974, the annual rate jumped to an average of about 14.0 per cent. A similar pattern was demonstrated in the rural areas where for the 1956-1966 period, the average annual rate was about 3.1 per cent, increasing to 15.1 per cent for the 1967-1974 period. When compared to the pattern for all consumer items, Figure 2 shows that both the relative price levels and the actual rates of increase have been consistently higher for food and drink, particularly since about 1969-1970. Although the rate of increase in the rural areas has been a sustained one since 1968, with a marked rise since 1972, increases in the Kingston area have been relatively moderate through 1971, but since then, the rate has almost become equal to that for the rural areas.

Equations 2.0 and 2.1 show that for both the Kingston and rural areas the pattern of movement in import prices has an appreciable effect on food and drink prices.

$$2.0 \quad \text{Kingston:} \quad D = 15.35 \quad - 45.62 \ w/_y \quad + 1.12 \ p^m$$
$$\qquad\qquad\qquad\qquad\qquad (-1.17) \qquad\qquad (3.66)\ ^*$$

$$R^2 \quad = \quad 0.80$$
$$Se \quad = \quad 4.91$$
$$D\text{--}W \quad = \quad 2.42$$

$$2.1 \quad \text{Rural:} \quad D = 35.24 \quad - 14.89 \ w/_y \quad + 1.43 \ p^m$$
$$\qquad\qquad\qquad\qquad\qquad (-0.29) \qquad\qquad (3.15)\ ^*$$

$$R^2 \quad = \quad 0.65$$
$$Se \quad = \quad 6.40$$
$$D\text{--}W \quad = \quad 1.91$$

As in the case of the price movements for all consumer items, the effect of labour cost is of some relevance to food prices. There is however no concrete

FIGURE 2:   RELATIVE MOVEMENT OF PRICES FOR FOOD AND
                         FOR ALL ITEMS

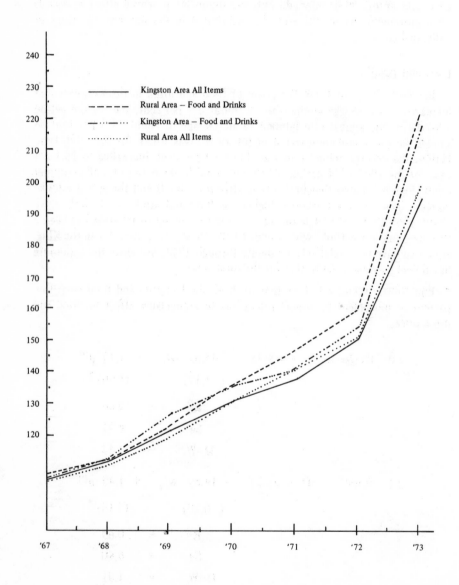

evidence to suggest that the overall increase in food prices for both the Kingston and rural areas has been appreciably affected by this variable.

In the case of the rural areas, the level of mark-up in food prices is shown in equation 3.0 to be much greater than for the Kingston area. The estimates show that for a ten per cent increase in import prices, we would expect about a 1.4 per cent increase in the rural retail price level. As one would normally expect, there are many service charges, particularly transportation and handling which would invariably serve to affect rural price levels and the movement of these levels. For purposes of this analysis, the category food and drinks consists of eight sub-categories, but the statistical explanation of price movements was possible only for three of these sub-categories. These are fresh meat and fish (D^{mf}), bread, cereal and sugar (D^{bc}), and beverages and other food items (D^{bo}). Table 3 presents the pattern of price changes in these items through December 1974.

The statistical difficulty of capturing the behaviour of prices for the remaining five sub-categories, which consists of tinned meats, dairy products, fats and oils, starchy fruits and vegetables, and other non-starchy fruits and vegetables may be attributed to at least four factors, or a combination of these factors. These would include the fact that these prices are not subject to the influence of variables on which the general model has been postulated; trading in these commodities does not take place totally within the framework of an organized market structure; the price determination process may for the most part exhibit an extreme *ad hoc* character, as would be the case where the price is a bargained compromise; the price is controlled by government, e.g., tinned meats, fats and oils.

Equations (3.0) through (5.1) present the respective estimates which have been generated for those items the price movements of which can be statistically explained.

$$\text{(3.0) Kingston:} \quad D^{mf} = -38.57 + 1.62\ p^m$$

$$(4.29)$$

$$R^2 = 0.71$$

$$Se = 9.57$$

$$D\text{--}W = 1.12$$

$$\text{(3.1) Rural:} \quad D^{mf} = -69.33 + 1.86\ p^m$$

$$(8.93)\ ^*$$

$$R^2 = 0.92$$

$$Se = 5.28$$

$$D\text{--}W = 0.98$$

(4.0) Kingston: D^{bc} = 79.68   − 92.90 w/y + 0.60 p^m

$$(-5.35)^* \qquad (3.84)^*$$

$$R^2 \quad = \quad 0.85$$

$$Se \quad = \quad 3.04$$

$$D{-}W \quad = \quad 2.75$$

(4.1) Rural: D^{bc} = 77.97   − 73.85 w/y + 0.54 p^m

$$(-4.60)^* \quad (3.77)$$

$$R^2 \quad = \quad 0.85$$

$$Se \quad = \quad 2.61$$

$$D{-}W \quad = \quad 2.23$$

Equation (5.0)   Kingston: D^{bo} = 70.73   − 31.64 w/y + 0.47 p^m

$$(-1.88) \quad (3.66)^*$$

$$R^2 \quad = \quad 0.67$$

$$Se \quad = \quad 2.86$$

$$D{-}W \quad = \quad 2.17$$

Equation (5.1)   Rural: D^{bo} = −8.63   − 83.56 w/y + 1.48 p^m

$$(-2.27)^* \quad (4.26)^*$$

$$R^2 \quad = \quad 0.74$$

$$Se \quad = \quad 0.62$$

$$D{-}W \quad = \quad 1.93$$

It is clearly demonstrated from the above estimates that the effect of import prices is quite strong on the movement of the prices of the sub-categories in question. In general, these prices as well as those for all goods tend to be consistently higher and to increase at a relatively faster rate in rural areas than in the Kingston area.

Most firms involved in the production and distribution of bread, cereal and sugar depend on relatively high inputs of labour, and this serves to explain the significance of the labour cost variable for this particular category of commodities in both Kingston and the rural areas (see equations 4.0 and 4.1).

Non-Food Items[21]

The statistical explanation of the pattern of price formation for most of these

TABLE 3

AVERAGE ANNUAL CHANGE IN PRICES FOR SELECTED FOOD ITEMS

| | PERCENTAGE INCREASE | | | | | |
| | KINGSTON AREA | | | RURAL AREA | | |
Item	1957–1966	1967–1973	Overall Average (1957–1973)	1957–1966	1967–1973	Overall Average (1957–1973)
Fresh Meat & Fish	5.60	15.2	5.2	5.6	14.5	4.8
Bread, Cereal & Sugar	1.70	12.4	5.2	1.30	12.9	5.0
Beverages & Other Food Items	1.50	12.7	5.1	3.20	11.1	5.3
All Foods and Drinks (D)	4.4	12.5	4.6	4.9	12.8	4.9

items has not been as efficient as in the cases of the aggregative index and the index for food items. Many of the sub-categories in this group had to be eliminated in view of the difficulty in developing reasonable arguments from the data which are available on prices and on other relevant explanatory variables.[22] For convenience, the more important categories and the estimates obtained are presented in Table 4 for both the Kingston and rural areas. It is obvious from the Table that the most important variable influencing the prices of those categories for which reasonably efficient statistical estimates could be generated, is import prices. The labour cost variable is important for some categories, noticeably clothing, household expenses and medical expenses. The estimates for this particular variable have however been very unstable and do not really provide a sufficiently dependable basis for extrapolations or direct policy simulations.

CONCLUSION

An attempt has been made in this study to identify and assess the main forces behind the determination of market prices in the Jamaican economy. The investigation is essentially based on the mark-up model of pricing. There are, however, a number of limitations, most of which relate to statistical problems resulting from the unavailability of high quality data. For example, some of the variables such as the profit rate, industry wage rates, etc. which *a priori* would be postulated to be of much importance in the price formation process, could not be examined in as much detail as would be desirable. Primarily, the study reveals that the two most important factors influencing price determination in Jamaica are import prices, and the long-run normal labour cost in an industry. Supply variations which result in market imbalances have also been examined, but were found to be of minor importance for most commodities.

Apart from the direct causative effects of the major explanatory variables, there are a number of important indirect effects which must be recognized in order to more fully understand the mechanics of price determination in the Jamaican economy. In a situation where the rate of expansion of local productive capacity is relatively low, particularly in the capital goods sector, the movement of domestic prices becomes invariably locked into market conditions prevailing in foreign markets. This is usually further exacerbated by an insufficiently diversified export sector. The main components of this sector, agriculture, bauxite and alumina are essentially supply inelastic. In cases of increased export earnings, which invariably give rise to improved real incomes in the short term, there is the definite tendency for an upward pressure on imports. If the levels of output for consumer goods do not accompany increased income levels, or if the increased incomes are not creamed off for capital expansion, not only will imports increase, but prices will inevitably rise due to the excess demand which has been created. Furthermore, if price levels are generally higher and rising faster in the foreign markets from which purchases are made this will only serve to further worsen the domestic inflating trend.[23]

TABLE 4: STATISTICAL ESTIMATES FOR SELECTED NONFOOD ITEMS

Category And Geographic Area	ESTIMATES & SAMPLING ERROR			EFFICIENCY INDICATORS			COMMENTS
	CONSTANT	w/y	p^m	R^2	Se	D-W	
MEDICAL EXPENSES							
Kingston Area	2.20	0.34 (3.14)		0.47	0.04	0.68	These estimates were based on the logarithmic transform of the variables.
Rural Area	2.16	0.27 (2.30)		0.32	0.04	1.02	
CLOTHING							
Rural Area	113.13	-81.79 (-1.97)	0.44 (1.80)	0.35	4.07	1.16	Estimates for Kingston were unstable and non-consistent.
CLOTHING MATERIAL							
Kingston Area	107.3	-112.3 (-1.74)	0.66 (3.15)	0.50	2.80	1.64	
Rural Area	74.1	-49.8 (-34.9)	0.59 (20.46)	0.46	3.42	1.06	
FOOTWEAR							
Kingston Area	70.78	12.26 (0.20)	0.23 (3.31)	0.63	4.17	1.51	Estimates for rural area were statistically unsatisfactory.
HOUSEHOLD EXPENSES							
Kingston Area	50.51	12.25 (1.09)	0.40 (10.77)	0.93	1.10	1.80	
Rural Area	68.03	-47.74 (-3.14)	0.64 (11.40)	0.95	2.06	2.00	

Another very important factor involves the rationalization of programmes which seek to expand local productive capacity. In cases where the emphasis is placed on non-agricultural production, as was the case during the 1960s for example, the result will naturally be higher levels of non-farm incomes. This policy posture serves not only to discourage agricultural production and encourage a transfer of resources from this sector, but also to create an environment in which food prices are continually bidded up along with long-run normal farm costs.[24] There is usually a continuing effort through public sector intervention to maintain parity between the farm and non-farm sectors.

Although it would have been more desirable to study the role of costs in determining prices from data which are assembled at the level of the firm, the approach involving broad industry wage shares which is used in this study has been quite revealing. As has been earlier recognized, though the wage share represents an important variable in price formation, it does not seem to have been a primary factor in influencing the upward trend in prices in the Jamaican economy for the period reviewed. It has however been noted that this might not be true of all industries, or for firms within industries. A major deficiency of this study results from the fact that adequate data were not available to facilitate a detailed assessment of the movement in relative shares, i.e. including wages, rents, dividends and profits at the industry level. Table 5 however presents the pattern in the movement of these shares with respect to national income for the period 1959-74. All factor shares with the exception of corporate profits have either been relatively stable over the period, or have declined. The most noticeable decline has been non-corporate business income, particularly the non-farm component.

Although these have not been empirically revealed in the study, there seems to be two important features which are likely to characterize pricing decisions by many firms. The first is the tendency to stipulate and maintain as a matter of policy a minimum profit margin. The result of this is that increased (actual) costs, much of which might not become a part of long-run normal costs give rise to adjustments in prices which ensure that prior profits are not decreased.[25] The second important feature is the fact that the organized workforce in the respective industries is not as a general rule cognizant of the basic aspects of production and distribution. There is therefore no relation between the motivation and operations of trade unions and the market mechanism. This often results in unduly lengthy wage negotiating, or wage settlements which do not realistically relate to increased real marginal output. The activities of trade unions serve to further aggravate the problem by disregarding inter-industry differences in productivity, and in many instances, the tendency is to enforce standard guidelines as regards percentage increases in wages. It is therefore necessary for trade unions to more fully appreciate the basic principles of the market system as they relate particularly to production and distribution, and educate the workforce (members and non-members) accordingly.

This study serves to introduce the importance of the need to have a fuller understanding of the mechanics of price determination. Certain important limit-

TABLE 5: THE PATTERN OF RELATIVE FACTOR
SHARES FOR SELECT PERIODS

(Per cent)

FACTOR	YEAR			
	1959	1962	1968	1974
EMPLOYEE COMPENSATION	59.4	60.1	61.4	58.6
WAGES AND SALARIES	58.0	58.5	59.7	56.5
CORPORATE PROFITS	9.9	10.7	13.0	21.0
DIVIDEND INCOME	0.5	0.7	0.7	0.4
RENTAL INCOME	3.0	3.2	2.7	2.3
NET INTEREST	5.0	4.8	4.6	5.6
NONCORPORATE BUSINESS INCOME	22.5	20.9	17.3	11.7
NONFARM	16.1	15.2	12.7	7.4
FARM	6.4	5.7	4.6	4.3

Source: National Income and Products Account, Dept. of
Statistics, Jamaica.

ations have been recognized. However a number of insights are provided, and it is hoped that further attempts (particularly through survey work), will be made to build on these. Further work in this regard is of much importance, since there needs to be a fuller understanding of the role of market prices and the importance of price stability in the pursuance of such objectives as an increased rate of economic development and growth which is socially acceptable, and improvements in such target variables as employment and production.

FOOTNOTES

1.   The author wishes to register his appreciation for the support provided by the ISER without which this project might not have been completed. The ideas expressed in

this paper are exclusively those of the author and do not necessarily reflect the position of any organization or institution with which he is associated.

2. It is empirically possible to generate a series of inter-industry purchases from a standard input-output model, and this would make possible the development of a series on value-added prices. An example of this exercise of relating market prices to value added prices is demonstrated by Fisher et. al. in the Brookings model of the United States [7]. The basic assumption of intertemporal constancy in prices and productivity would however be too stringent for an economy which is experiencing structural changes under inflationary conditions, as is the case for Jamaica.

3. In the case of short-run analyses, the factor which is of prime concern is that which goes to labour (wages). Capital stock as a factor input is assumed to be fixed and does not influence pricing decisions for profit maximization. That share which goes to capital is considered to be quasi-rent and is subsumed under short-run costs.

4. The assumption here is that other variable costs such as distribution costs are subsumed in these categories.

5. A detailed development is beyond the scope of this investigation.

6. For an interesting discussion of these problems, see Afriat [1].

7. Since January 1975, three sets of indices are being produced, for Kingston, other main towns, and the rural areas.

8. External factors such as changes in international exchange rates are included under the general role of costs.

9. Variations in productivity levels and in physical inventory are directly related to output considerations and will be independently examined.

10. An excellent manifestation of this phenomenon followed the December 1971 devaluation of the U.S. dollar. The resulting fall in the parity ratio of the U.S. dollar to the Jamaican dollar in effect reduced the cost of imports from the United States. In many cases, however, domestic prices were not voluntarily adjusted to reflect this fall in cost and for some commodities had to be forced down by government fiat.

11. The appropriate base should be normal output, which could be estimated in several ways, including: (a) a moving average of actual output, (b) seasonally adjusted actual output, and (c) an extrapolation over time of full capacity output. None of these will be possible either because of the short series of output data available, or the lack of information on output capacity by industries at each point in time.

12. It has been strongly alleged, but not empirically verified that there were much *ad hoc* mark-ups in retail prices on such occasions as after the 1969 decimalization of the Jamaican currency, in cases of currency devaluation, and even unjustifiably during periods of inflation as experienced during 1973-74.

13. The parenthesized symbol associated with each item will be used later to represent the dependent variable in the structural definition of the respective price-equations to be estimated.

14. All equations have been estimated by the ordinary least squares regression procedure. The parenthesized value which subtends each statistical estimate represents the student's t-ratio. A starred estimate indicates that it is statistically significant at the 95 per cent probability level. The other indicators of goodness-of-fit are respectively symbolised as R^2 = coefficient of determination, Se = standard error of the

estimate, and D-W = the Durbin-Watson statistic for serial correlation in the residuals. Both R^2 and Se are corrected for the number of degrees of freedom.

15. It is a commonly held opinion among economists that inflation is usually a characteristic of the economic development and growth process in market economies.

16. A more detailed inter-industry analysis of this aspect of price formation is necessary before a full assessment of this particular phenomenon can be made. This is beyond the scope of the present analysis.

17. Some alternative specifications were estimated and the coefficient for the import index has consistently ranged from 0.80 to 0.92 for Kingston and 0.76 to 0.80 for rural area. Manhertz [14] has estimated a coefficient of 0.90 for the effect of import prices on domestic prices for the economy as a whole, but Hines [11] has found that no significant relationship exists.

18. The classification of industrialised countries used here conforms to that which is used by the International Monetary Fund, and includes the United States, the United Kingdom, Belgium, Denmark, France, Italy, the Netherlands, Norway, Canada and Japan.

19. Earlier years were not used due to the base change of the index and the tediousness of undertaking a satisfactory adjustment, as earlier pointed out.

20. One such factor to which price increases have been attributed in Jamaica is the decimalization of the currency in September 1969. There is, however, no clear empirical evidence to substantiate that particular phenomenon.

21. This category has been consolidated from items 3-7 as outlined above in section 4.0.

22. As earlier observed one approach to solving this particular problem is to undertake the collection of primary data from which the mechanics of pricing by the firm can be more clearly studied. The study by Lanzioletti [13] provides an example of this approach.

23. Much of the Jamaican experience during the period 1972-74 could be attributed to a combination of the above factors.

24. This kind of imbalance could also characterize the relationship between consumer goods and producer goods industries.

25. One important contributor to this phenomenon is periodic changes in the financing of credit. For example, short to medium term financing is usually arranged for long-term capital expansion, resulting in relatively high servicing costs to be met from current operations. The margin on the firm's product is thereby increased accordingly.

REFERENCES

[1]   Afriat, Sidney, *International Comparisons of Prices and Output,* National Bureau of Economic Research, New York 1972.

[2]   Ando, A. and F. Modigliani, "Econometric Analysis of Stabilization Policies". *American Economic Review,* Papers and Proceedings, May 1969.

[3]   Brewster, H., "Wages, Prices and Productivity Relations in Jamaica 1957-62", *Social and Economic Studies,* Vol. 17, No. 2 June 1968.

[4]   Bronfenbrenner, Martin, and Franklyn Holzman, "Survey of Inflation Theory", *American Economic Review,* Vol. 52, September 1963.

[5]   Duesenberry, J.; O.A. Eckstein, and G. Fromm, "A Simulation of the U.S. Economy in Recession", *Econometrica,* October 1960.

[6]   Eckstein, Otto, "A Theory of the Wage-Price Process in Modern Industry", *Review of Economic Studies,* Vol. 31, 1964.

[7]   Fisher, Franklin, "Dynamic Structure and Estimation in Economy-wide Econometric Models" in the *Brookings SSRC Quarterly Econometric Model of the United States,* Chapter 15, North-Holland 1965.

[8]   Gordon, R.A., "Different Changes in Prices of Consumer and Industrial Goods", *American Economic Review,* December, 1961.

[9]   Hall, Marshall, "An Analysis of the Determinants of Money Wage Changes in Jamaica, 1958-64", *Social and Economic Studies,* Vol. 17, No. 2 June 1968.

[10]   Harris, Donald J., "Saving and Foreign Trade as Constraints in Economic Growth", *Social and Economic Studies,* Vol. 19,   No. 2, June 1970.

[11]   Hines, A.G., "Incomes, Prices and Productivity in Jamaica", *Mimeo,* Delivered to the Symposium on Prices and Incomes Policy, National Planning Agency, Jamaica, August 1973.

[12]   Klein, Lawrence R. and R.J. Ball, "Some Econometrics of the Determination of Absolute Prices and Wages", *Economic Journal,* September 1959.

[13]   Lanzioletti, R., "Pricing Objectives in Large Companies", *American Economic Review,* December 1958.

[14]   Manhertz, Huntley G., "An Exploratory Econometric Model for Jamaica, *Social and Economic Studies,* Vol. 18, No. 2, June 1971.

[15]   Maynard, Geoffrey, *Economic Development and the Price Level*, Macmillan, 1962.

[16]   Nerlove, Marc, *The Dynamics of Supply: Estimation of Farmers' Response to Price*, Baltimore: Johns Hopkins Press, 1958.

[17]   Richardson, G.B., "Demand and Supply Reconsidered", *Oxford Economic Papers*, June 1956.

[18]   Yance. J., "A Model of Price Flexibility", *American Economic Review*, June 1960.

WALLACE JOEFIELD-NAPIER

INFLATION, INFLATIONARY EXPECTATIONS AND MONETARY BEHAVIOUR IN JAMAICA

INTRODUCTION[1]

The objective of this paper is to focus attention on one of the major problems which Jamaica faces today, that is, inflation.

Although several statements have been made in the local press and in other seminars about the high rate of inflation that has been evident in Jamaica for over the last two decades, so far few rigorous attempts had been made to identify and isolate the real causes of the inflationary spiral.[2] It has been felt by economists both in Government and University circles that the inflationary spiral in Jamaica has been caused by an increase in the money supply. An expansion in the money supply had the effect of increasing effective demand at a period when there was a relative decline in productivity in the Jamaican economy.

While not disagreeing with the preceding view, other economists felt that too great an emphasis was placed on increases in the money supply. They held the view that the inflationary spiral was due in the main to rapid increases in the cost of production which were passed on to consumers. The high incidence of cost inflation was attributed to two factors: firstly, to an exhorbitant increase in the local wage bill due to vigorous trade union bargaining and secondly, to too rapid increases in the price of raw material inputs and food which were mainly imported.

A final school of economic thought in Jamaica held the view that the inflationary spiral in Jamaica has been mainly due to the structural imbalances that originated in the colonial era and still persist today. It is important to note that cost inflation is thought of as a specific form of structural inflation with the cost push being initiated in the modern sector of the Jamaican economy and later being transmitted to the traditional sector.

It is of utmost importance to determine whether or not inflation in Jamaica has been caused by the excessive wage demand of trade unions, or by much too rapid increases in public expenditures or by rapid price increase in metropolitan economies, in addition to the structural rigidities which are inherent in the Jamaican economy.

The focus of this paper, however, is not on the above contributory factors. Instead, attention is directed to some often neglected aspects of Caribbean inflation. To be more specific, the objective of our exercise is three-fold; firstly, to analyse the trend in consumer prices in Jamaica over the period 1959-1972; secondly, to analyse the actual and expected rates of inflation over the same period;[3] and thirdly, to investigate the effects of inflation on money demand.

TREND ANALYSIS OF JAMAICA INFLATION

In order to investigate the movements in domestic consumer prices, both inter-temporarily and spatially, we decided to utilise the existing data on consumer price indices as published by the Department of Statistics. These indices pertained to both Rural and Urban Jamaica. Because a high degree of aggregation bias is likely to exist in annual data, the quarterly data series were utilised.

The analysis was then undertaken over the two time periods which we felt would capture most adequately the significant changes in prices that had occurred both in the pre-1967 and post-1967 devaluation periods. The first period extends from the first quarter 1959 to the fourth quarter 1967, while the second period commences in the first quarter 1968 and concludes in the fourth quarter, 1972. Growth rates were calculated for each of the major commodity groupings included in the consumer price index using both the linear and geometric trend approaches. The results obtained are given in Table A1 in the Appendix.

As indicated by the figures given in the Table, the rate of growth of the All Item Price Index for Kingston over the period first quarter 1959 to the fourth quarter 1972 was rapid, averaging 0.97 per cent per quarter. That this rapid increase was not due to an increase in wage rates as a consequence of aggressive trade union bargaining is evident from the fact that the rate of growth of the wage index was significantly lower than that of the All Item Urban Index, being 0.74 per cent per quarter. This is also shown on Table A1.

While it is felt in some quarters that the rapid increase in prices in an inflationary situation is dampened by an increase in imports, this does not seem to be the case in Jamaica; instead, we feel that the rapid increases in imports as indicated by a growth rate in the quarterly import index of 0.98 per cent may have been responsible for a large proportion of the domestic price increases.

Turning now to the components of the All Item price index in the Urban Area (KMA), we see that there existed a great deal of variation between these components. In this context, it is interesting to note that the rate of growth per quarter of the various components of the All Item Index over the whole sample period were as follows:-

	Per Cent
Food and Drink	0.97
Housing	0.92
Household Furnishing	0.50
Clothing	0.77

Personal Expenses   1.37
Transportation   1.97

Judged by the coefficient of variation, the greatest fluctuation seemed to have occurred in clothing (.019) closely followed by housing (.015), food (.014) and fuel (.012).

With respect to the sub-period analysis of the Urban Price Index, the estimates of growth rates indicated that the prices of all of the components of the All Item Index grew at a much more rapid rate during the period, fourth quarter 1967 — fourth quarter 1972, when compared with the earlier period, first quarter 1959 to third quarter, 1967. It is shown that while the price of food and drink in Kingston rose by only 0.57 per cent per quarter between first quarter 1959 and fourth quarter 1967, the growth rate more than doubled between the fourth quarter of 1967 and the fourth of 1972. In the latter period, the growth rate of food and drink increased by approximately 1.95 per cent per quarter. A tendency towards a two to four-fold increase in the rate of growth of prices as between the both periods was also evident in the cases of fuel and housing. In the case of personal expenses and clothing the increases were not as significant varying from 1.25 per cent to 1.32 per cent and from 0.55 per cent to 1.00 per cent respectively. A notable exception to this pattern, however, was the price of household furnishing whose growth rate actually fell from 1.60 per cent in the first period to 0.85 per cent in the post-1967 period.

To a large extent the results obtained for food, fuel and housing were expected since a high proportion of these commodities were imported and Jamaica had devalued in 1967. The most plausible explanation for the trend in household furnishing seems to be the fact that the various governments of Jamaica had been pursuing vigorous policies of industrialization since the early 1950s, and it is precisely industries such as those producing household furnishings which were mainly nurtured. The net effect of these policies then seemed to be an increase in the supply of those commodities on the domestic market and a subsequent lowering of prices.

The pattern of high rates of growth in the prices of food and clothing which was evident in Kingston also seemed to have persisted in rural areas of Jamaica. This is shown by the figures in Table A2 of the Appendix. In this context, it is interesting to note that while the retail price index for food and fuel in the Kingston area grew at the rate of 0.98 per cent and 0.97 per cent, for Rural Areas, the rates of growth were 1.77 per cent and 0.92 per cent respectively. The rapid rate of growth in the price of fuel in Rural Areas could have been both the cause and effect of increases in the cost of transportation. However, in the case of food, inasmuch as Jamaica has always been predominantly agricultural, a large proportion of households should supply themselves with a large part of the food they consume. If so, then the impact of any increases in the prices of imported food items ought not to be felt by these households. That this was not the case seems to indicate that much of rural consumption requirements are not supplied directly from rural output.

Looking at the other components of the All Item Rural price index, we see that the rate of growth of clothing was 0.90 per cent as compared to 0.77 per cent in the Kingston area. For housing and household furnishing the growth rates were 0.71 per cent and 0.65 per cent respectively. In fact, for almost all commodity groups, except fuel and personal expenses, the rural growth rates were higher than those in Kingston. In the case of the All Item Rural index, the rate of growth (by the geometric definition) was also higher than in Kingston being 1.04 per cent as compared to 0.97 per cent in the latter location (KMA).

The coefficients of variation indicate that the commodity group 'fuel' experienced the greatest fluctuation being followed by clothing and personal expenses, both having coefficients of variation of .0146. The coefficients of variation for the different commodities over the sub-periods again indicated that the prices of non-durables, such as food, were rather more stable than those of durables, for example, housing.

Comparing the variations in all commodity groupings over the entire period of analysis we can only conclude that their persistent variation may be nothing more than a reflection of the inherent instability of the Jamaican economic structure as well as the social system.

In terms of the intra-period growth rates our calculations indicated that the rates of growth of the All Item Price Index and its components were consistently lower in the pre-1967 devaluation period. Thus we see that while for the period first quarter 1959 to third quarter 1967, the rates of growth of food, fuel, clothing, housing and household furnishing were 0.83, 0.36, 0.64, 0.64 and 0.39 respectively, in the period fourth quarter 1967 to fourth quarter 1972, the rates of growth were 2.03, 1.77, 1.74, 0.81 and 1.17 respectively.

So far our analysis of the trends in consumer prices in Jamaica has been based on data obtained from the various household budget surveys undertaken by the Department of Statistics. To a large extent the weights used and hence the results obtained were largely determined by the prices of the various commodities which were included in the basket of goods selected by the Department of Statistics as being representative of the items chosen by an average Jamaican household.

An apparent shortcoming of this approach stems from the fact that in Jamaica, the practice has been to select the representative household from the lower income stratum of the Jamaican society. To all intents this practice may have been. valid in the pre-1950 era when incomes in the Jamaican society may not have been as sophisticated as they were over the period of our analysis. The argument is usually put forth that inasmuch as households of the lower income groups form the bulk of consumers in Jamaica any index derived from commodities purchased by these households must be truly representative. There is some merit in this argument but the major factor that militates against its unqualified acceptance is the fact that lower income consumers may indulge in forms of expenditure which may be mainly associated with people in higher income groups. To the extent that the latter type of consumer does not provide information on his expenditures to the enumerator, some commodities may be given very low weights in the construction of the price index. Thus a major limitation of the existing Jamaican consumer price indices seems to be in their exemption of certain categories of consumers, notably, consumers within high income groups.

THE ACTUAL AND EXPECTED RATES OF INFLATION[4]

Notwithstanding the apparent shortcoming of both the rural and urban consumer price indices, we utilised the urban index for the computation of actual and expected rates of inflation over the period 1 January 1959 to 31 December 1972. For the calculation of the expected rate of inflation we made the assumption that Jamaican consumers had some notion of what future price increases were derived from their past experiences of price increases. Since the expected rate of increase in prices was not an observable variable we resorted to the use of a proxy variable[5] introduced into the literature by Fisher [5], [6], and extensively utilised by Cagan [2].

Cagan in his seminal work on hyper-inflation assumed that the expected rate of change of prices is revised per period of time in proportion to the difference between the actual rate of change in prices and the rate of change that was expected. The relationship between the expected rate of change in prices and actual price can be expressed as:

$$E_t = (1 - e^{-B}) \sum_{i=o}^{\infty} C_{t-i} \; e^{-Bi} \qquad (1)$$

or

$$E_t = (1 - e^{-B}) \; C_t + (e^{-B}) E_{t-1} \qquad (2)$$

Where E_t represents the expected rate of inflation in any given month; C_t, the current rate of inflation in the current month; E_{t-i}, the expected rate of inflation in the preceding month; B, the coefficient of expectation and e, the base of the natural logs.[6]

In addition, it may be noted that i the horizon is assumed to be settled in some period in the past and this facilitates setting the initial value of the expected rate of inflation to zero. In so far as the coefficient of adjustment (B) is concerned, this is the constant of proportionality in the basic assumption. Essentially, the value of the coefficient of expectation indicates the speed with which expectation adjusts to changes in the actual rate of increases in prices.

From this one can also infer that the higher the coefficient of expectation the higher will be the proportion of current prices considered in the expectations formed by economic agents. It is customary when forming the expectation variable to utilise 1/B periods, but in general the coefficient of expectation must not exceed 10 for at this value the expected rate of change is equal to the actual. rate of change in prices.

Because we feel that prices in the Rural Areas of Jamaica are to a large extent determined by Urban price changes, our analysis of the rates of inflation in Jamaica was based solely on the data from the Urban Price series. In order to compute the expected rate of inflation, we applied Equation 1 to the current rate of change of prices commencing in January 1956 (that is, a horizon of three years was utilised). The derived series are given in Table 1.

TABLE 1

EXPECTED RATE OF INCREASE IN PRICES KINGSTON 1959-1972 JAMAICA COEFFICIENT OF EXPECTATION 1959-70

Year	Rate of Change in Prices	0.2	0.4	0.6	0.8	1.0	1.2	1.4	1.6
				EXPECTED RATE OF CHANGE IN PRICES					
1959	.259	.382	.364	.334	.291	.284	.251	.237	.214
1960	.242	.389	.337	.314	.298	.285	.276	.269	.263
1961	.076	.974	.498	.320	.233	.184	.153	.133	.119
1962	.076	.156	-.027	- .058	- .068	- .072	- .074	- .075	- .075
1963	.151	.547	.332	.254	.218	.197	.185	.176	.171
1964	.043	1.560	.989	.769	.633	.584	.538	.506	.483
1965	- 035	.388	.187	.131	.101	.081	.069	.060	.054
1966	.150	.792	.389	.272	.226	.202	.189	.180	.173
1967	.241	1.566	.761	.476	.351	.290	.259	.243	.231
1968	.176	- 3.271	-2.366	-1.625	1.117	- .769	- .527	- .355	- .231
1969	.509	6.211	4.461	3.274	2.503	1.984	1.623	1.363	1.173
1970	.315	2.660	1.205	.833	.666	.569	.506	.461	.429
1971	.805	3.470	2.132	1.634	1.377	1.219	1.115	1.042	1.039
1972	.645	3.903	2.067	1.467	1.182	1.021	.919	.851	1.541

The results indicate that the actual rate of inflation fluctuated widely over the period 1959 to 1972. Nevertheless, the period 1960 to 1966, was one of marked decline in the inflationary spiral, reaching an all time low of 0.035 points per month for 1965. The estimates also indicated that there was a sharp increase in the rate of inflation between 1966 and 1967 (from 0.150 to 0.241 points per month) but by 1968 this rate of increase fell by almost one half. A possible explanation may be the long delivery lags for imported goods which prevented an instantaneous adjustment of domestic prices to devaluation.

However, by 1969 the full brunt of the impact of the price increases brought about by the devaluation seemed to have been absorbed by the Jamaican economy, the net effect of this being a sharp increase in domestic price levels

(.509 points per month) during the year. By 1970 the rate of inflation exhibited a fall but this was only short-lived for by 1971 it rose again to an all time high of .805 points per month. At the end of our period of analysis, that is, 1972, the rate of inflation dropped slightly from its peak of 0.805 to 0.645 points per month.

As will be observed in Table 1, there exist different values of expected rates of inflation for each of the coefficients of adjustment chosen, hence it is difficult to ascertain which is the most appropriate expected rate of inflation for a given time period. To guide our choice of optimal expected rate of inflation, we resorted to both economic theory and statistical procedures. According to the theory of the demand for money, the expected rate of inflation is a determinant of money demands. We therefore regressed the real cash balance on the expected rates of inflation associated with different coefficients of expectation, and then chose as optimal that coefficient of expectation (and hence expected rate of inflation) which gave the highest coefficient of determination (R^2).

We utilised the following functional relationship:

$$M/Y = e^{-aE+b} \tag{3}$$

Where M is real money stock,

Y is real output, and

E is the expected rate of inflation.

The above equation indicates that the demand for real cash balances per unit of real output is a function of the expected rate of change of prices per month. By a further process of linearization, that is, by taking log transforms of the basic equation, the estimating equation was then obtained as:

$$\log M/Y = -a E + b \tag{4}$$

where 'a' and 'b' are the intercept term and slope coefficient respectively.

Because different empirical definitions of the money stock may lead to different results, three definitions of money stocks (MS I, MS II, MS III)[7] were regressed on the expected rate of inflation. The three best results in terms of low standard errors and high R^2 were chosen for each of the variants of money stock as well as the different values of the adjustment coefficient for real cash balances.

In order to investigate whether or not the coefficients of adjustment shifted over time it is also necessary that we investigate the movement between the rate of inflation and real cash balances in the sub-periods. However, because we had to resort to the use of annual data, the limited number of observations at our disposal prevented such an approach.

As indicated by the results in Table 2, the first variant of the real cash balances when regressed on the various expected rates of inflation did not give a good fit as evidenced by the low R^2 and high degree of serial correlation. For example, with a coefficient of adjustment of .02 the value of the coefficient of the explanatory variable 'E' was statistically significant at the 10 per cent level, but when we increased the coefficient of adjustment it led to a further decrease in the explanatory power of the various equations. In other words, an increase in the coefficient of adjustment from .02 to 1.2 and 1.6 led to a fall in the explanatory power of the estimated equations to 0.472 and 0.531 respectively. The poor fit between the first variant of the real cash balance and the expected rate of inflation is not too unreasonable when we consider that the coefficient of adjustment that we chose may have been significantly different from the true coefficient of expectation. On the other hand the variation may have been due to the fact that there were other variables not included in our model which affected the demand for real cash balances.

We then proceeded to use a more expansive variant of the real cash balance, that is, MS II. The results obtained from fitting this variant of real cash balance to the various expected rates of inflation were better. For example, when we utilised a coefficient of expectation of .02 the expected rate of inflation explained over 90 per cent of the variation in the real cash balance. The high explanatory power of the functional form chosen was also evident when larger coefficients of adjustments were utilised. When the coefficient of adjustment was increased from .02 to 1.2 and 1.6 then our estimated equation explains 68.4 per cent and 74.4 per cent respectively, of the variation in real cash balances.

In the case of the third variant of real cash balances the use of a coefficient of adjustment of .02 also gave a good fit as indicated by the high values of R^2 as well as the Durbin-Watson 'D' statistic. However, the explanatory power of the estimated equations fell as the coefficients of adjustment were increased from .02 to 1.2 and 1.6. When the coefficient of adjustment is 1.2, the estimated equation explains only 59.0 per cent of the variation in real cash balance; however, when the adjustment coefficient is increased to 1.6 the explanatory power of the equation correspondingly falls to 58.2 per cent.

As a result of our plotting the adjusted coefficients of multiple determination against the corresponding value of the coefficient of adjustment, we decided that the optimal value of the latter coefficient exists when B = .02. In other words, our 'goodness of fit' criterion indicated that the expected rate of inflation series derived by assuming B = 0.2 explains a larger proportion of the variation in the dependent variable than any other configuration of the coefficient of adjustment; hence it was chosen as the best fitting series.

The magnitude of the coefficient of expectation (.02) clearly indicated that the average length of weighting patterns was a little more than four years (50 months). A comparison of the expected series generated by the above coefficient with the actual rate of inflation series gives a rough indication of the overall effect of price expectations in the Jamaican inflationary process. Observe (Table 1) for example, that over the period of analysis the expected series was invariably greater in magnitude than the actual series; the only exception being 1968. Also, the turning points in the expected series occurred later than those in the actual series. In column II, we have reported the differences in

TABLE 2

RESULTS SIMPLE REGRESSIONS OF THE LOGARITHM OF THE VALUE OF THE MONEY STOCK PER UNIT OF OUTPUT (M/Po) ON THE EXPECTED RATE OF INFLATION (E)

Money Stock	Regression Equation					R^2	S_e	D.W.	Elasticity of M/Po with respect to E
(M/Po) I									
(B = 0.2)	$(M/Po)_I$	=	2.087	−	0.324 E (.131)	0.582	.109	0.714	+.457
(B = 1.2)	$(M/Po)_I$	=	2.137	−	0.135 E (.073)	0.472	.119	.344	+.499
(B = 1.6)	$(M/Po)_I$	=	2.148	−	0.136 E (.063)	0.531	.114	0.514	+.413
(M/Po) II									
(B=0.2)	$(M/Po)_{II}$	=	2.042	−	0.928 E	0.910	.102	1.442	+2.337
(B = 1.2)	$(M/Po)_{II}$	=	1.967	−	0.359 E (.110)	0.684	.181	1.161	+.751
(B = 1.6)	$(M/Po)_{II}$	=	1.934	−	0.351 E (.145)	0.744	.165	1.425	+.750

(contd.)

TABLE 2 *(continued)*

Money Stock	Regression Equation			R^2	S_e	D.W.	Elasticity of M/Po with respect to E
(M/Po) III							
(B=0.2)	$(M/Po)_{III} = 1.504$	$-$	.997 E (.192)	.832	.161	1.747	+ 2.406
(B=1.2)	$(M/Po)_{III} = 1.413$	$-$	0.364 E (.144)	.590	.235	1.190	+ .756
(B=1.6)	$(M/Po)_{III} = 1.239$	$-$	0.322 E (.157)	.582	.236	1.342	+ .721

Mean value of C.E. = 0.2; 1.2; 1.4; 1.6.
Expected rate of inflation 1.409; .392; .364; .399.

both series. It can be observed that while both series showed considerable variation over the period of analysis, the actual rate of inflation ranging from -.035 points to .805 points and the expected rate of inflation from -3.271 to 6.211 points, the differences were much more consistent, ranging from -3.447 points to 3.258 points.

Together, the preceding factors indicated that price expectation effects did not have an instantaneous impact upon domestic price formation, but filtered its way through the economy. In addition, the above analysis indicated that the Jamaican consumer was pessimistic so far as government price control policies were concerned.

THE VELOCITY OF MONEY AND THE RATE OF INFLATION

It has been recognised that one of the major factors influencing the rate of inflation has been the velocity of money. The relationship between these two variables can simply be described as one wherein any increases in the velocity of money lead to an acceleration in the rate of inflation, and conversely a fall in money velocity has the opposite effect.

Implicit in such a relationship, however, is the notion that small increases in prices will not effect the velocity of money appreciably, while, on the other hand, significant changes in the rate of inflation can and do lead to significant changes in money and this can be measured. In a situation of rapid increases in prices it will be relatively unattractive for an individual to hold cash balances *vis-à-vis* assets held in other forms. However, any switch from nominal to real cash balances must of necessity lead to a bidding up of prices and a corresponding increase in the velocity of money.

So far it has not been shown whether there is a significant relationship between the velocity of money and the rates of change in prices in Jamaica. This type of analysis has been undertaken in many countries. For example, Cagan investigated the incidence of hyper-inflation in seven European countries after World War I and during World War II. His study centred on the relationship between velocity of money and the expected rate of inflation. Our aim at this point in the study will be to examine the relationship for Jamaica. The discussion is based on the regression results presented in Section II, and on the data in Tables 3 and 4.

The evidence as presented in Table 4, indicates that up to 1960, the M_1/Y ratio rose quite rapidly as per capita income rose, but over the succeeding years the ratio exhibited a great deal of fluctuation despite the continuing upward trend in per capita income.

To some extent the wide fluctuation in the income velocity of circulation associated with the M_1/Y ratio, can be explained by the fact that during periods of buoyant export prices, domestic income reacted almost instantaneously, whereas the commercial banks, being in the main branches of metropolitan banks, tended to be cautious and passive in their operations, in which case there

TABLE 3

JAMAICA, GROSS NATIONAL PRODUCT, MONEY STOCK & INCOME VELOCITY OF CIRCULATION OF MONEY SUPPLY 1959-1972

(JA $ MILLION)

Year	G.N.P. at factor cost	Money Stock I	Money Stock II	Money Stock III	Income Velocity of M1	Income Velocity of M2	Income Velocity of M3
1959	384.1	56.2	60.8	100.2	6.8	6.3	3.8
1960	415.0	63.2	65.8	111.8	6.6	6.3	3.7
1961	443.2	59.4	66.2	112.0	7.5	7.0	3.9
1962	463.5	51.8	61.6	112.1	8.9	7.5	5.1
1963	494.4	54.8	70.9	129.6	9.0	7.0	3.8
1964	531.7	61.1	79.7	149.7	8.7	6.7	3.5
1965	575.5	62.7	82.4	162.4	9.2	7.0	3.5
1966	626.6	65.6	89.7	179.5	9.5	7.0	3.5
1967	671.2	71.0	102.0	203.2	9.4	6.9	3.3
1968	738.6	85.1	127.3	245.8	8.7	5.8	3.0
1969	816.0	107.8	162.2	306.0	7.6	5.0	2.7
1970	921.7	116.8	194.7	323.3	7.9	4.7	2.8
1971	987.7	131.4	242.0	424.2	7.2	4.1	2.3
1972	1090.9	158.3	290.0	501.2	6.9	3.8	2.2

Sources: (1) Department of Statistics: *Abstract of Statistics,* various issues.

(2) *Bank of Jamaica Report,* various issues.

was a tendency towards restraint in the use of bank money. In other words, during such periods (periods of boom in the export sector) the public demand for very active cash balances was greater than the supply, and this led to an increase in the velocity of circulation. The converse was also true.

Comparing the movement of the M_2/Y ratio or K_2 $(M_2 = M_1 + TD)$[8] with that of income per capita, it shows that M_2/Y rose, though marginally, over the first two years of the period being reviewed, but fell in the two succeeding years. The fluctuation in M_2/Y continued up to 1966, but thereafter the trend in M_2/Y was markedly upwards. In as much as time deposits increased as the monetization of the economy increased, the upward trend in the M_2/Y ratio

TABLE 4

JAMAICA: INDEX NUMBERS FOR SELECTED SERIES 1959-1972 (1967 = 100)

YEAR	Index of Money Stock I	Index of Money Stock II	Index of Money Stock III	Index of Real Output	Index of Money Stock per Unit of Output	Index of the Real Value of M.S.I. Per Unit Output	Index of Money Stock per Unit of Output	Index of the Real Value of M.S.II Per Unit Output	Index of Money Stock Per Unit of Output III	Index of Real Value of M.S.III Per Unit Output
1959	79.1	59.6	49.3	69.9	113.2	138.4	85.3	101.9	70.5	86.2
1960	89.0	64.5	55.0	73.9	120.4	143.8	87.3	104.3	74.4	88.9
1961	83.7	64.9	55.1	75.9	110.3	126.8	85.5	98.3	72.6	83.4
1962	72.9	60.4	55.2	77.8	93.7	105.5	77.6	87.4	71.1	80.1
1963	77.2	69.5	63.8	80.5	95.9	104.8	86.3	94.3	79.2	86.5
1964	86.0	78.1	73.7	87.1	98.7	108.6	89.7	98.7	78.8	86.7
1965	88.3	80.8	79.9	93.5	94.4	102.9	86.4	94.2	85.4	93.1
1966	92.4	87.9	88.3	96.3	95.9	99.0	91.3	94.2	85.4	93.1
1967	100.0	100.0	100.0	100.0	100.0	100.0	100.0	100.0	100.0	100.0
1968	119.8	124.8	121.0	104.2	115.0	108.9	119.8	113.4	116.1	109.9
1969	151.8	159.0	150.6	110.4	137.5	124.9	144.0	130.8	136.4	123.9
1970	164.5	190.9	159.1	119.0	138.2	119.8	160.4	139.0	133.7	115.9
1971	185.1	237.2	208.7	124.6	148.5	125.7	190.4	161.2	140.5	119.0
1972	222.9	284.3	246.6	133.8	166.6	137.1	170.6	140.4	148.0	121.8

* Based on the official estimates of GNP in 1967 prices.

in the post-1966 era indicated not only an increase in the holding of cash balances for transaction, but also an increase in the public holdings of time deposit as a store of value. Second, due to perturbations in the international economy and their subsequent influence on the Jamaican economy through the bauxite, tourism and banking sectors, exogenous impulses had a great impact on the level of domestic economic activity. As income fluctuated within the afore-mentioned sectors of the economy the importance of time deposits moved in sympathy. This meant that in certain critical years (1962 and 1967), the ele-. ment of cash balance for transaction purposes within M_2/Y dominated the store of value element.

Turning now to a comparison of the M_3/Y ratio and per capita income, it can be observed in Table 4 that there was less fluctuation in this ratio when compared to M_1/Y and M_2/Y ratios as income rose. In fact, only over the first four years of the period being reviewed did the M_3/Y ratio exhibit a small degree of fluctuation, but in the subsequent years the series exhibited a perceptible upward trend. The upward trend in the M_3/Y ratio clearly indicates that the high deposit rate after 1965 had the stimulating effect of inducing much more positive savings habits within the Jamaican economy.

Another possible interpretation may have been the widespread and increasing tendency to hoard cash induced by the financial uncertainty that developed after 1967. Such as interpretation seems to be valid when one looks at the figures in Table 4, for the data clearly show that after 1967 there was steady fall in the velocity of circulation associated with the M_3/Y ratio. This finding also implies that after 1967 there was a growth in the precautionary demand for money (hedging against liquidity) which prevailed over any tendency towards a movement into goods (hedging against purchasing power deterioration).

Furthermore, the trend in the M_3/Y ratio also seems to indicate that money illusion remained strong enough to preclude any development of hyper-inflation. Thus, hoarding had a stabilising effect on the monetary situation in that it damp-ened the effect of a rapidly rising money supply on the price level and money income. Implicitly, increased taxation of households can be seen as an attempt to forestall the inflationary threat that was being posed by the increased monetary hoards.

The time series of Treasury bill rates (Fig. 1) which highlight the movement of interest rates within the Jamaican money market, show that the interest rate rose rapidly up to 1962, fell in 1963-64 and fluctuated at a high level in 1965 and subsequent years. The influence of the interest rate on M_1/Y can be said to be insignificant up to 1960 because of its relatively low level. However, in the post-1960 years the increases in interest rates may have led people to hold less cash balances and so caused the M_1/Y ratio to decline.

Correspondingly, the fluctuations in the interest rate did not seem to have affected the M_2/Y ratio between 1959 and 1972; instead the Jamaican govern-ment policies, initiated after 1962, of limiting the overseas investment of insti-tutional savers had the stimulating effect of attracting more time deposits and hence caused M_2/Y to rise. The insignificance of the interest rate coefficients in the empirical analysis substantiated this argument.[9] While the influence of the interest rate on M_3/Y did not seem to be significant before 1965, increases in the deposit rate after that year may have been instrumental in enhancing the attractiveness of savings deposits, and this in turn may have led to an increase in the M3/Y ratio.

There was an inflationary pressure within the Jamaican economy in the 1950s, due to rapid expansion of the mining sector. The boom in manufacturing and tourism sectors in the early 1960s accentuated the upward movement in consumer prices and prices increased further by the devaluation of sterling in 1967. From 1967 onwards, increases in prices remained virtually unchecked. Theoretically, people's expectation of rising prices may cause them to 'economize' in the use of their cash balance, thus causing the M_1/Y ratio to fall. But conclusive evidence does not exist on the influence of price movements on M_1/Y. In so far as the influence of price movements on M_2/Y and M_3/Y is concerned, the following interpretation seems tenable: the inflationary pressures within the Jamaican economy in the post-1959 era caused people to deposit less in time and savings deposits and this in turn caused M_2/Y and M_3/Y to be smaller than they normally would have been.

Next, we turn to the statistical analysis of the relationship between the expected rate of inflation and the three variants of real cash balances. Recall that in the previous section we chose as being optimal that expected rate of inflation series that had a coefficient of adjustment of 0.2. A careful evaluation of the empirical result obtained by regressing the most active variant of cash balance, M_1/Y, on this series clearly reveal that there occurred a shift, though not significant, from cash to real assets within the Jamaican economy over the period 1959 to 1972. The coefficient of E was statistically significant. Furthermore, as the result showed, the demand for M_1/Y with respect to the expected rate of inflation was inelastic: inelastic in the sense that a one per cent increase in the expected rate of inflation led to a 0.457 per cent increase in real cash balances. This tendency of a shift towards real assets within the Jamaican economy was further substantiated by the results obtained when we regressed the less active variants of cash balances, M_2/Y and M_3/Y, on the optimal rate of inflation. The coefficients of determination were high, being .910 and .832 respectively. While the coefficients of the expected rate of inflation were theoretically correct as well as being statistically significant, the mean expected rate of inflation of 1.409 gave elasticities of demand for real cash balances per unit of output of 1.308 and 1.405 respectively.

In the existing literature, a similar study has been undertaken by Campbell [4], using both South Korean and Brazilian data. Comparing with his results, we found that our results seem to be very reasonable. In this context, Campbell found that during the period of relatively low rates of inflation in Brazil (1948-1957), the best coefficient of expectation was 2 per cent. The elasticity of demand for the most active form of real cash balance per unit of output (M_1/Y) with respect to the expected rate of inflation that he obtained, was

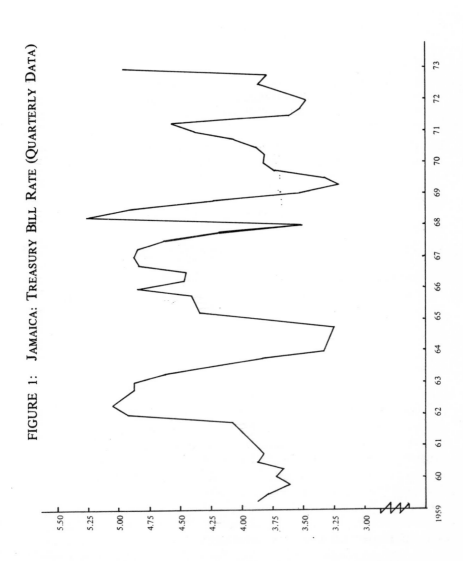

FIGURE 1:   JAMAICA: TREASURY BILL RATE (QUARTERLY DATA)

slightly less than that which was derived in this study (that is, .319).

At this point it may be noted that the elasticities we estimated for the more expansive variants of real cash balance (M_2/Y and M_3/Y) seemed to be somewhat lower than expected, but we were unable to check the consistency of these estimates with Campbell's work as his analysis was confined to the most active variant of real cash balance.

For comparison, the real cash balance elasticities implied by Campbell's estimates, are presented below:

TABLE 5

Elasticities of the Index of the Real Value of the Money Stock Per Unit of Output (M/Y) With Respect To The Mean Expected Rate of Inflation (E)

SOUTH KOREA:	January 1953-June 1961 (102 months) (1953 = 100)					
	Min.M_1/Y	Max.M_1/Y	Mean M_1/Y	Min.E	Max.E	Elasticity
	73.2	255.2	168.0	2.77	6.88	.421
BRAZIL:	January 1948-December 1957 (120 months) (1953 = 100)					
	Min.M_1/Y	Max.M_1/Y	Mean M_1/Y	Min.E	Max. E	Elasticity
	97.3	112.0	95.2	.74	1.04	.319

Source: Campbell [4]

Finally, in an attempt to guage the effect of both per capita income and the domestic rate of interest (Treasury Bill rate) on real cash balances, the model was extended to include these variables.[10] Serious auto-correlation was evident in the error term of each of the equations that we estimated. Moreover, the computed coefficients of both variables were found to be insignificantly different from zero. These results seem to indicate that per capita income and domestic interest rate had a negligible influence on the income velocity of money.

SUMMARY AND CONCLUDING REMARKS

Several tentative conclusions can be drawn from our analysis.

First, we have observed that the per cent rate of increase in prices within the Jamaican economy was quite rapid over the period 1959-1972, and a major contributory factor was the rapid increase in the price of imports.

Second, the disaggregated approach in analysing the trend in prices is superior to the aggregate approach in terms of revealing the items that were mainly responsible for the increases in the cost of living.

With the disaggregated approach, we have shown that increases in the prices of transportation and personal expenses were the most rapid. Similarly, our analysis indicated that price increases were more rapid in rural areas as compared to urban areas.

Third, while Cagan pointed out the importance of price expectation in the context of hyper-inflation, we considered additionally the role of expectations during periods of modest inflation within an underdeveloped economy, namely, Jamaica. We found that over the 14 years that were considered, the optimal rate of price expectations occurred when the coefficient of adjustment was .02 which means that the Jamaican consumer does have some notion about price increases and acts accordingly. Although we do not have any measurement of the impact of the media on expectation formation, it seems reasonable to assume that the improvements in communication since the late 1950s have contributed immensely to the formation of expectations.

Fourth, the income velocity of circulations of money appeared to have fluctuated widely since 1959 and this was especially the case with the most active form of real cash balances, M_1/Y. Given the upward trend in per capita income over the same period, the fluctuations in the velocity of circulation of money (narrowly defined) suggest that over time per capita income has a negligible effect on the velocity of circulation of this form of money. Our findings for money defined in the broad sense M3 (M2 + SD) lend support to Friedman's theory that 'money' is a luxury good — as real income rises, M would rise more rapidly than nominal income or M3/Y would rise.

Finally, the statistical analysis of the relationship between real cash balances and the expected rate of inflation indicated that there was a movement from cash to real assets during the period 1959-1972. It should be mentioned, moreover, that the movement seemed to be great since the price elasticity of demand for all variants of cash balances, except M1/Y, was well above unity.

FOOTNOTES

1. I would like to thank my colleague Compton Bourne for his helpful comments and suggestions.

2. See for example, the earlier empirical contributions on Jamaican inflation by Brewster [1], Hall [9], and Hines [10].

3. To be sure, the earlier contributions do not analyse the implications of expectations. In other words, the basic underlying framework of the existing studies on Jamaican inflation do not give recognition to the fact that expectations may have a profound influence on the rate of inflation.

4.   While the analysis of inflation has been couched in partial equilibrium terms in this paper, it must be recognised that the analysis can be undertaken in a general equilibrium framework.

5.   For a description of various techniques of estimating expected variables, see Nerlove [11].

6.   Equation (2) is an alternative and perhaps easier way of deriving equation (1).

7.   Where MS1 = Currency plus Demand Deposits at Commercial Banks; MSII = MSI plus Time Deposits; MSIII = MSII plus Savings Deposits.

8.   In the definition(s), of the more expensive variants of money supply, T.D. denotes time deposits and S.D. indicates savings deposits.

9.   Inasmuch as both the Treasury Bill rate and per capita real income variables were statistically insignificant, the estimated equation was not presented in this paper.

10. Despite the fact that many studies have been undertaken on the relationship between inflation and interest rates, no single explanation has gained widespread credence. See for example, Friedman [7], Cagan and Gandolfi [3], Gibson [8], Yohe and Karnosky [12].

REFERENCES

1.   Brewster, H., "Wage Price and Productivity Relations in Jamaica, 1957-1962", *Social and Economic Studies,* Vol. 17, No. 2, 1968.

2.   Cagan, P., "The Monetary Dynamics of Hyper-Inflation" in M. Friedman (ed.), *Studies in the Quantity Theory of Money,* Chicago, 1956.

3.   _____ and Gandolfi, A., "The Lag on Monetary Policy as Implied by the Time Pattern of Monetary Effects on Interest Rates, *American Economic Review,* Vol. 59, 1969.

4.   Campbell, C., "The Velocity of Money and the Rate of Inflation: Recent Experiences in South Korea and Brazil" in D. Meiselman (ed.), *Varieties of Monetary Experience,* Chicago, 1970.

5.   Fisher, I., *Mathematical Investigation in the Theory of Value and Prices,* bound with *Appreciation and Interest,* N.Y. Kelley, 1961.

6.   _____ , *The Theory of Interest,* 1st ed., 1930, reprinted, New York: Augustus M. Kelley, 1961.

7.   Friedman, M., "Factors Affecting the level of Interest Rates" in *Proceedings of the Conference on Savings and Residential Savings, 1968.*

8.   Gibson, W.E., "Price Expectations Effects on Interest Rates", *Journal of Finance,* Vol. 25 March 1970.

9.   Hall, M., "An Analysis of the Determinants of Money Wage Changes in Jamaica", *Social and Economic Studies,* Vol. 17 No. 2, 1968.

10. Hines, B., "Wages and Price formation in the Jamaican Economy, 1956-1972". Govt. of Jamaica Planning Unit, 1972.

11. Nerlove, M., "Distributed Lags and Demand Analysis", *Agricultural Handbook* No. 141 U.S. Department of Agriculture, 1958.

12. Yohe, W. and Karnosky, D., "Interest Rates and Price level changes 1952-1969", *Federal Reserve Bank of St. Louis Review*, December, 1969.

APPENDIX

STATISTICAL TABLE A1 (KINGSTON METROPOLITAN AREA)

FOOD AND DRINK (K.M.A.) — 1st Qr. 1959-4th Qr. 1972

Linear Trend	$77.2491 + 1.0976t$	S.E. =	.9997
		C.V. =	.0166
Geometric Trend	$80.7814 \ (1.0098)^t$	S.E. =	0.8671
		C.V. =	0.0144
		G.R. =	0.98

FUEL (K.M.A.) — 1st Qr. 1959-4th Qr. 1972

Linear Trend	$76.6340 + 1.0622t$	S.E. =	0.9157
		C.V. =	0.0158
Geometric Trend	$79.9045 \ (1.0097)^t$	S.E. =	0.7951
		C.V. =	0.0137
		G.R. =	0.97

HOUSING (K.M.A.) — 1st Qr. - 4th Qr. 1972

Linear Trend	$76.2485 + 0.9168t$	S.E. =	0.8305
		C.V. =	0.0151
Geometric Trend	$77.7742 \ (1.0092)^t$	S.E. =	0.8116
		C.V. =	0.0148
		G.R. =	0.92

HOUSEHOLD FURNISHING (K.M.A.) — 1st Qr. 1959 - 4th Qr. 1972

Linear Trend	$86.9094 + 0.5162t$	S.E. =	.4313
		C.V. =	.0075
Geometric Trend	$87.5921 \ (1.0050)^t$	S.E. =	0.4158
		C.V. =	.0072
		G.R. =	0.50

CLOTHING (K.M.A.) — 1st Qr. 1959 - 4th Qr. 1972

Linear Trend	$79.7751 + 0.8034t$	S.E. =	1.0591
		C.V. =	0.0190
Geometric Trend	$81.5929 \ (1.0077)^t$	S.E. =	1.0232
		C.V. =	0.0183
		G.R. =	0.77

PERSONAL EXPENSES (K.M.A.) — 1st Qr. 1959 - 4th Qr. 1972

Linear Trend	$64.4505 + 1.4007t$	S.E. = 0.5202 C.V. = 0.0090
Geometric Trend	$68.9562 \ (1.0137)^t$	S.E. = 0.3549 C.V. = 0.0061 G.R. = 1.37

ALL ITEMS (K.M.A.) — 1st Qr. 1959 - 4th Qr. 1972

Linear Trend	$76.9881 + 1.0541t$	S.E. = 0.8621 C.V. = 0.0145
Geometric Trend	$80.0794 \ (1.0097)^t$	S.E. = 0.7459 C.V. = 0.0125 G.R. = 0.97

FOOD AND DRINK (K.M.A.) — 1st Qr. 1959 - 3rd Qr. 1967

Linear Trend	$85.7280 + 0.5423t$	S.E. = 0.4265 C.V. = 0.0132
Geometric Trend	$85.9992 \ (1.0057)^t$	S.E. = 0.4233 C.V. = 0.0131 G.R. = 0.57

FOOD AND DRINK (K.M.A.) — 4th Qr. 1967 - 4th Qr. 1972

Linear Trend	$103.7454 + 2.4497t$	S.E. = 0.7389 C.V. = 0.0275
Geometric Trend	$104.9248 \ (1.0195)^t$	S.E. = 0.7994 C.V. = 0.0297 G.R. = 1.95

FUEL (K.M.A.) — 1st Qr. 1959 - 3rd Qr. 1967

Linear Trend	$84.3004 + 0.5655t$	S.E. = 0.4046 C.V. = 0.0127
Geometric Trend	$84.4194 \ (1.0061)^t$	S.E. = 0.4253 C.V. = 0.0133 G.R. = 0.61

FUEL (K.M.A.) — 4th Qr. 1967 - 4th Qr. 1972

Linear Trend	$101.9852 + 2.3748t$	S.E. = 0.4572 C.V. = 0.0182
Geometric Trend	$103.3712 \ (1.0190)^t$	S.E. = 0.4199 C.V. = 0.0167 G.R. = 1.90

HOUSING (K.M.A.) — 1st Qr. 1959 - 3rd Qr. 1967

Linear Trend	$78.2695 + 0.8066t$	S.E. = 1.1884 C.V. = 0.0530
Geometric Trend	$77.9172 \ (1.0093)^t$	S.E. = 1.2218 C.V. = 0.0545 G.R. = 0.93

HOUSING (K.M.A.) – 4th Qr. 1967 - 4th Qr. 1972

Linear Trend	101.1060 + 1.6155t	S.E. =	0.2845	
		C.V. =	0.0115	
Geometric Trend	101.6848 $(1.0139)^t$	S.E. =	0.3325	
		C.V. =	0.0135	
		G.R. =	1.39	

HOUSEHOLD FURNISHING (K.M.A.) – 1st Qr. 1959 - 3rd Qr. 1967

Linear Trend	88.7733 + 0.4017t	S.E. =	0.5299	
		C.V. =	0.0115	
Geometric Trend	101.6848 $(1.0139)^t$	S.E. =	0.3325	
		C.V. =	0.0135	
		G.R. =	1.39	

HOUSEHOLD FURNISHING (K.M.A.) – 1st Qr. 1959 - 3rd Qr. 1967

Linear Trend	88.7733 + 0.4017t	S.E. =	0.5299	
		C.V. =	0.0158	
Geometric Trend	88.7791 $(1.0042)^t$	S.E. =	0.5359	
		C.V. =	0.0160	
		G.R. =	1.60	

HOUSEHOLD FURNISHING (K.M.A.) – 4th Qr. 1967 - 4th Qr. 1972

Linear Trend	100.8528 + 0.9423t	S.E. =	0.3569	
		C.V. =	0.0154	
Geometric Trend	101.1481 $(1.0085)^t$	S.E. =	0.3443	
		C.V. =	.1149	
		G.R. =	0.85	

CLOTHING (K.M.A.) – 1st Qr. 1959 - 3rd Qr. 1967

Linear Trend	82.4085 + 0.6611t	S.E. =	1.4952	
		C.V. =	0.0469	
Geometric Trend	83.3004 $(1.0065)^t$	S.E. =	1.4896	
		C.V. =	0.0467	
		G.R. =	.65	

CLOTHING (K.M.A.) – 4th Qr. 1967 - 4th Qr. 1972

Linear Trend	98.2203 + 1.7355t	S.E. =	1.7737	
		C.V. =	0.3966	
Geometric Trend	99.1251 $(1.0150)^t$	S.E. =	0.3284	
		C.V. =	.0135	
		G.R. =	1.00	

PERSONAL EXPENSES (K.M.A.) – 1st Qr. 1959 - 3rd Qr. 1967

Linear Trend	69.0076 + 1.077t	S.E. =	0.4122	
		C.V. =	.0159	
Geometric Trend	70.0164 $(1.0125)^t$	S.E. =	.4340	
		C.V. =	.0166	
		G.R. =	1.25	

PERSONAL EXPENSES (K.M.A.) — 4th Qr. 1967 - 4th Qr. 1972

Linear Trend	111.9558	+ 1.7087t	S.E. =	0.4870	
			C.V. =	0.0180	
Geometric Trend	112.7445	$(1.0132)^t$	S.E. =	0.4452	
			C.V. =	0.0164	
			G.R. =	1.32	

ALL ITEMS (K.M.A.) — 1st Qr. 1959 - 3rd Qr. 1967

Linear Trend	84.0025	+ 0.5574t	S.E. =	0.5521	
			C.V. =	0.0168	
Geometric Trend	84.1179	$(1.0064)^t$	S.E. =	0.5661	
			C.V. =	0.0172	
			G.R. =	0.64	

ALL ITEMS (K.M.A.) — 4th Qr. 1967 - 4th Qr. 1972

Linear Trend	103.4982	+ 2.2177t	S.E. =	0.3762	
			C.V. =	0.0142	
Geometric Trend	104.6740	$(1.0178)^t$	S.E. =	0.3639	
			C.V. =	0.0138	
			G.R. =	1.78	

STATISTICAL TABLE A2 (RURAL AREAS)

FOOD AND DRINK (RURAL) — 1st Qr. 1959 - 4th Qr. 1972

Linear Trend	70.5182	+ 1.2764t	S.E. =	0.9315	
			C.V. =	0.0159	
Geometric Trend	75.0275	$(1.0117)^t$	S.E. =	0.7	
			C.V. =	.0126	
			G.R. =	1.77	

FUEL (RURAL) — 1st Qr. 1959 - 4th Qr. 1972

Linear Trend	80.1973	+ 1.0497t	S.E. =	1.0830	
			C.V. =	0.0189	
Geometric Trend	83.5715	$(1.0092)^t$	S.E. =	0.9593	
			C.V. =	0.0168	
			G.R. =	0.92	

HOUSING (RURAL) — 1st Qr. 1959 - 4th Qr. 1972

Linear Trend	82.1456	+ 0.7206t	S.E. =	0.5059	
			C.V. =	0.0088	
Geometric Trend	83.3259	$(1.0071)^t$	S.E. =	0.4980	
			C.V. =	0.0087	
			G.R. =	0.71	

HOUSEHOLD FURNISHING (RURAL) – 1st Qr. 1959-4th Qr. 1972

Linear Trend	$83.1306 + 0.6814t$	S.E. =	0.6100
		C.V. =	0.0107
Geometric Trend	$84.5372 \ (1.0065)^t$	S.E. =	0.5587
		C.V. =	0.0098
		G.R. =	0.65

CLOTHING (RURAL) – 1st Qr. 1959 - 4th Qr. 1972

Linear Trend	$75.3398 + 0.9508^t$	S.E. =	0.9172
		C.V. =	0.0161
Geometric Trend	$78.1716 \ (1.0090)^t$	S.E. =	0.8296
		C.V. =	.0146
		G.R. =	0.90

PERSONAL EXPENSES (RURAL) – 1st Qr. 1959 - 4th Qr. 1972

Linear Trend	$68.8750 + 1.1372t$	S.E. =	0.8972
		C.V. =	0.0163
Geometric Trend	$71.3628 \ (1.0116)^t$	S.E. =	0.8024
		C.V. =	0.0146
		G.R. =	1.16

ALL ITEMS (RURAL) – 1st Qr. 1959 - 4th Qr. 1972

Linear Trend	$73.7958 + 1.1107t$	S.E. =	0.8387
		C.V. =	0.0149
Geometric Trend	$77.2336 \ (1.0104)^t$	S.E. =	0.6980
		C.V. =	0.0124
		G.R. =	1.04

FOOD AND DRINK (RURAL) – 1st Qr. 1959 - 3rd Qr. 1967

Linear Trend	$78.4842 + 0.7577t$	S.E. =	0.3762
		C.V. =	0.0142
Geometric Trend	$79.0783 \ (1.0083)^t$	S.E. =	0.3639
		C.V. =	0.0138
		G.R. =	0.83

FOOD AND DRINK (RURAL) – 4th Qr. 1967 - 4th Qr. 1972

Linear Trend	$103.4173 + 2.5963t$	S.E. =	0.6049
		C.V. =	0.0234
Geometric Trend	$104.9647 \ (1.0203)^t$	S.E. =	0.2947
		C.V. =	.0092
		G.R. =	2.03

RURAL (RURAL) – 1st Qr. 1959 - 3rd Qr. 1967

Linear Trend	$90.5466 + 0.3478t$	S.E. =	0.6049
		C.V. =	0.0234
Geometric Trend	$90.6505 \ (1.0036)^t$	S.E. =	0.5931
		C.V. =	0.0023
		G.R. =	0.36

FUEL (RURAL) – 4th Qr. 1967 - 4th Qr. 1972

Linear Trend	107.1878 + 2.2888t	S.E. =	0.6835
		C.V. =	0.0250
Geometric Trend	108.4277 $(1.0177)^t$	S.E. =	0.6544
		C.V. =	0.0239
		G.R. =	1.77

HOUSING (RURAL) – 1st Qr. 1959 - 3rd Qr. 1967

Linear Trend	84.1376 + 0.5836t	S.E. =	0.4900
		C.V. =	0.0153
Geometric Trend	84.1755 $(1.0064)^t$	S.E. =	0.5161
		C.V. =	0.016
		G.R. =	0.64

HOUSING (RURAL) – 4th Qr. 1967 - 4th Qr. 1972

Linear Trend	105.8705 + 0.9267	S.E. =	0.9829
		C.V. =	0.0406
Geometric Trend	105.9600 $(1.0081)^t$	S.E. =	1.0000
		C.V. =	0.0413
		G.R. =	0.81

HOUSEHOLD FURNISHING (RURAL) – 1st Qr. - 1959 - 3rd Qr. 1967

Linear Trend	87.7590 + 0.3742t	S.E. =	0.5710
		C.V. =	0.0174
Geometric Trend	87.8359 $(1.0039)^t$	S.E. =	0.5693
		C.V. =	0.0175
		G.R. =	0.39

HOUSEHOLD FURNISHING (RURAL) – 4th Qr. 1967 - 4th Qr. 1972

Linear Trend	101.2961 + 1.3489t	S.E. =	0.3042
		C.V. =	0.0133
Geometric Trend	101.8547 $(1.0117)^t$	S.E. =	0.2630
		C.V. =	0.0115
		G.R. =	1.17

CLOTHING (RURAL) – 1st Qr. 1959 - 3rd Qr. 1967

Linear Trend	81.1761 + 05822t	S.E. =	0.2483
		C.V. =	0.0083
Geometric Trend	81.5029 $(1.0064)^t$	S.E. =	1.5262
		C.V. =	0.0082
		G.R. =	0.64

CLOTHING (RURAL) – 4th Qr. 1967 - 4th Qr. 1972

Linear Trend	97.7129 + 2.1129t	S.E. =	1.5262
		C.V. =	0.0558
Geometric Trend	99.3335 $(1.0174)^t$	S.E. =	1.4654
		C.V. =	0.0536
		G.R. =	1.74

PERSONAL EXPENSES (RURAL) – 1st Qr. 1959 - 4th Qr. 1967

Linear Trend	$71.7776 + 0.9445t$	S.E. = 1.4774
		C.V. = 0.0525
Geometric Trend	$71.7990 (1.0112)^t$	S.E. = 1.4860
		C.V. = 0.0528
		G.R. = 1.2

PERSONAL EXPENSES (RURAL) – 4th Qr. 1967 - 4th Qr. 1972

Linear Trend	$105.1307 + 1.5545t$	S.E. = 0.3961
		C.V. = 0.0164
Geometric Trend	$105.8369 (1.0128)^t$	S.E. = 0.3485
		C.V. = 0.0144
		G.R. = 1.28

ALL ITEMS (RURAL) – 1st Qr. 1959 - 3rd Qr. 1967

Linear Trend	$80.7533 + 0.6538t$	S.E. = 0.5415
		C.V. = 0.0183
Geometric Trend	$81.0724 (1.0071)^t$	S.E. = 0.5415
		C.V. = .0183
		G.R. = 0.71

ALL ITEMS (RURAL) – 4th Qr. 1967 - 4th Qr. 1972

Linear Trend	$103.1593 + 2.1974t$	S.E. = 0.4275
		C.V. = 0.0163
Geometric Trend	$104.3350 (1.0174)^t$	S.E. = 0.4059
		C.V. = 0.0154
		G.R. = 1.74

IMPORT INDEX – 1st Qr. 1959 - 4th Qr. 1972

Linear Trend	$75.8726 + 0.9817t$	S.E. = 1.2293
		C.V. = .0184
Geometric Trend	$78.5281 (1.0098)^t$	S.E. = 1.1561
		C.V. = .0121
		G.R. = 0.98

Where   S.E. denotes the standard error

C.V. denotes the coefficient of variation

G.R. denotes the rate of growth

COMPTON BOURNE AND WILBERNE PERSAUD

FINANCIAL VARIABLES IN THE INFLATIONARY PROCESS: TWO CARIBBEAN CASES

INTRODUCTION

Unprecedented high rates of price inflation within recent years have served to redirect attention to the problem of inflation in Caribbean economies. Recent writings on the subject, e.g. Ally [1], Latibeaudiere [5], St. Cyr [8], Thomas [9] and Ramjeesingh [7], have concentrated on the analysis of generating factors. Not surprisingly, virtually no academic attention has been devoted to the development of anti-inflation policy, for at the present time the latter step would be very much a matter of shooting in the dark since no firm knowledge exists with respect to inflationary impulses and spread mechanisms.

This is not to say there has been a shortage of empirical studies. However, as a result of limitations in data, statistical technique and model specification, no definitive findings have been arrived at. Moreover, those studies focus primarily on real variables such as factor costs and incomes, with rather little attention being devoted to the role of financial variables.

This paper analyses the influence of selected financial variables on the rate of inflation in Jamaica and in Trinidad and Tobago over the period 1967 to 1974. Quarterly data are employed throughout. The primary statistical technique utilised is multiple regression analysis. The structure of the paper is as follows. Section I describes the behaviour of particular economic time series over the period as a kind of background to the model formulated in Section II. In Section III, various versions of a reduced-form model of price determination are applied to the data, and results are reported. Section IV is in the nature of a provisional conclusion.

FEATURES OF RECENT INFLATION
Trinidad and Tobago

From December 1966 to December 1974, the absolute level of prices in Trinidad and Tobago, as measured by the retail price index, nearly doubled itself. More than sixty per cent of the increase in prices occurred in the final two years. This signifies a much more rapid rate of inflation in the later years than in the earlier ones. While the average quarterly rate of inflation was approximately 1.2 per cent for the first quarter of 1967 to the last quarter of 1972, the average quarterly rate for 1973(1) to 1974(4) was roughly 4.8 per cent. The pace of price change also differed among the several subcomponents of the retail price index. The index for food expanded by more than 90 per cent, while for the others the percentage change was in the region of 35– 65 per cent.

The time pattern of several real and financial variables such as wages, money supply, bank credit, government debt, and import prices has been adduced by recent commentators (e.g. Ally [1]) as *prima facie* evidence in support of several versions of cost-push and demand-pull theories of price inflation. It is quite evident from Figures 1 and 2 that there was pronounced upward movement in the time series for net domestic credit by the banking system (NDC); the Gross Government Debt (GGD); Money Supply (MS) narrowly defined; the index of import prices; the weighted average index of export prices (FP) for Trinidad and Tobago's import suppliers; and wages. To a lesser degree the series for the exchange rate, (XCR) represented by the trade conversion factor, and the weighted average commercial bank loan rate also rose over time.

A closer examination of some of the time series reveals some parallelism between the movements of some of them on the one hand, and the retail price index on the other hand. Dealing first with the import price index, one observes that over the entire period, import prices rose by more than 500 per cent, the rate of increase being extremely rapid (15 per cent) in the final two years. The index of minimum wage rates rose at a much slower and more uniform rate, averaging 1.9 per cent for 1967-1972, and 2.5 per cent for 1973-1974. Thus while domestic retail prices nearly doubled, nominal wages increased by about 80 per cent, thereby implying a deterioration in real wage income. It is worthwhile to note that real wages declined at an even faster rate from 1973(1) to 1974(4).

A considerable expansion in the stock of nominal money supply, bank credit and gross government debt accompanied the upsurge in domestic retail prices. Money supply slightly more than doubled, gross government debt increased by 120 per cent and net domestic bank credit increased by slightly under 90 per cent from 1967(1) to 1971(4). With the exception of the money supply, the rate of expansion was faster for 1967-1972 than for 1972-1974. Specifically, the stock of money averaged a quarterly rate of increase of 2.5 per cent for 1967-1972, and 3.8 per cent for 1972-1974. On the other hand, net domestic bank credit while expanding at an average quarterly rate of 4.4 per cent for 1967-1972, declined at approximately the same rate over the remaining two years. Gross government debt expanded at a slightly slower rate over the last two years, as compared to 1967-1972.

Jamaica

Over the period January 1966 to December 1974, the absolute price level in Jamaica, as measured by the retail price index, more than doubled itself. The index moved from 104.0 in 1966 to 212.5 in 1974. Of note too is the fact that from the year 1971 the movement of the CPI went from 138.8 to 212.5 in the final three years – a movement of about 35 per cent. Paralleling the case of Trinidad and Tobago, a more rapid rate of inflation is in evidence for the later

FIGURE 1:   SELECTED FINANCIAL VARIABLES – TRINIDAD
AND TOBAGO 1967-74

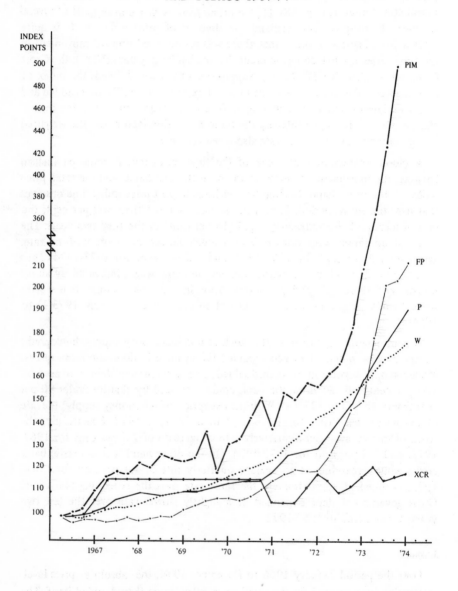

FIGURE 2:   SELECTED FINANCIAL VARIABLES — TRINIDAD
AND TOBAGO 1967-74

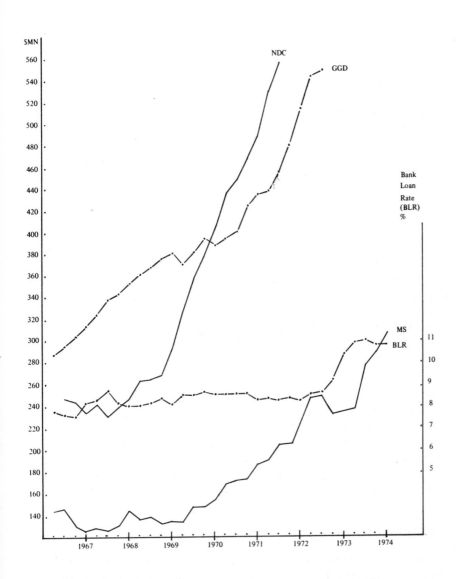

years. As expected, the rate of price change differed among the subcomponents of the index.

For the period 1967 to June 1974, the average quarterly rate of inflation was of the order roughly of 2.6 per cent. While for the period January 1967 to December 1972 the average quarterly rate of inflation was 1.7 per cent, that for the period January 1973 to June 1974 was of the order of 5.9 per cent — representing a much more rapid rate of increase in the last six quarters.

Along with this increase in prices the data point also to increases in import prices and other financial variables such as money supply, government debt, net domestic credit and bank credit. The time path of domestic and import prices (P and PIM respectively), the exchange rate (XCR), net domestic credit (NDC), bank loan rate (BLR), money supply (MS), and government deficit (GD), may be seen in Figure 3. Immediately striking is the cluster of the time paths of the money supply, domestic prices and import prices. So too are the fluctuations in government deficit, while it is noteworthy that the exchange rate has been reasonably stable. (In relation to the latter, note that balance of payments theory suggests trade-offs in movement as between the exchange rate, the price level and the level of reserves — given a small economy whose production levels and economic policy do not affect the rest of the world to any significant degree).

In all of this net domestic credit has been steadily climbing and the prime bank lending rate fluctuating as if (to the naked eye) systematically. The time patterns of behaviour charted above, lead to several questions as to the role of financial variables in the inflationary process in the two economies. For instance, what accounts for the cluster of the time paths of money supply, domestic and import prices — where does the line (or lines) of causation flow? What is the effect of fluctuating government deficit on the general level of prices? What of net domestic credit? Clearly there are relationships. What is not clear is the nature of these relationships.

Consider for instance the almost uniform movement of import prices, the money supply and the price level. Is this to be taken as evidence in support of the monetarist view that inflation is purely a monetary phenomenon? Alternatively is it that the money supply adjusts to the general level of prices? Indeed, both explanations could be true, though of course not simultaneously, unless one postulates some type of feedback mechanism. We need to be able to discriminate between the competing explanations that are possible.

THE MODEL OF PRICE DETERMINATION

Essentially theories of inflation fall broadly into two groups which one might call aggregate demand theories and cost push theories. In aggregate demand theories the focus is on price change as a market clearing mechanism, so that inflation is treated as a result of excess demand in factor and commodity markets. Within the aggregate demand genre, one can distinguish further between Keynesian theories which ascribe the main causal role to income disturbances,

FIGURE 3:   SELECTED FINANCIAL VARIABLES – JAMAICA 1967-74
EXCHANGE RATE (XCR) ON SEPARATE SCALE

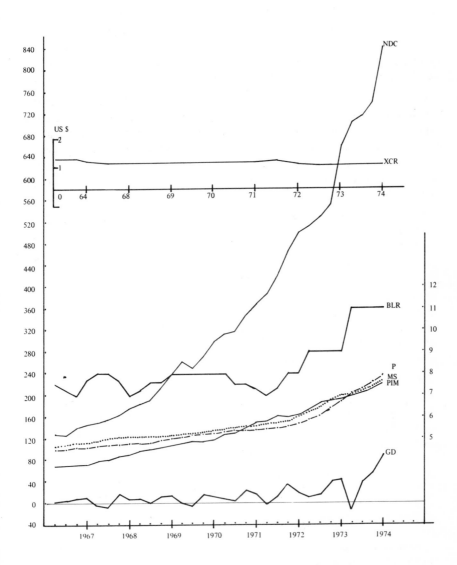

and Monetarist theories which treat the excess demand for money function as the central propulsive element in the inflationary process. Placed somewhat awkwardly between the strict Keynesian and strict Monetarist models are those models which focus on the credit and financial variables that augment demand in the consumption and investment markets.

Cost-push theories are centred around autonomous changes in the cost functions of 'production' enterprises. On the assumption of administered pricing of final products, inflation is viewed as the end result of factor prices rising faster than factor productivities. In the open, underdeveloped economy, labour and imported materials constitute high proportions of total costs. Not surprisingly, therefore, cost push models devote much attention to wages and import prices.

Research on inflation in the Caribbean so far has concentrated on wages and productivity relations, economic openness, government expenditures, taxes and disposable personal incomes. In this study, we are particularly interested in the propulsive role of monetary and financial variables. We do not purport to formulate a complete theory of inflation. Moreover, we adopt neither a purely aggregate demand nor a purely cost-push framework. Rather our formulation is a hybrid of both paradigms.

The basic structural model is summarised by the following system of fifteen equations:-

(1) $\quad \dot{P}_t = a_0 + a_1 \dot{W}_{t-i} + a_2 \dot{PIM}_{t-i} + a_3 \dot{BLR}_{t-i}$

$\qquad\qquad + a_4 \dot{ED}_{t-i} \qquad\qquad\qquad a_j > 0$

(2) $\quad \dot{ED}_t = \dot{Q}_t - \dot{E}_t$

(3) $\quad \dot{Q}_t = \dot{DO}_t - \dot{EX}_t + \dot{IM}_t$

(4) $\quad \dot{E}_t = \dot{C}_t + \dot{I}_t + \dot{G}_t$

(5) $\quad \dot{C}_t = c_0 + c_1 \dot{Q}_{t-i} + c_2 \dot{BLR}_{t-i} + c_3 \dot{NDC}_{t-i}$

$\qquad\qquad + c_4 (MS - MD)_{t-i} \qquad\qquad c_1, c_3, c_4 > 0$

$\qquad\qquad\qquad\qquad\qquad\qquad\qquad\qquad c_2 < 0$

(6) $\quad \dot{I}_t = \dot{I}_t^F + \dot{I}_t^P$

(7) $\quad \dot{I}_t^P = i_0 + i_1 (\dot{Q}_{t-i} - \dot{Q}_{t-i-1}) + i_2 (\dot{BLR}_{t-i} - \dot{BLR}_{t-i-1})$

$$+ i_3 (N\dot{D}C_{t-i} - N\dot{D}C_{t-i-1})$$

$$+ i_4 (M\dot{S}_{t-i} + M\dot{S}_{t-i-1} - M\dot{D}_{t-i} - M\dot{D}_{t-i-1})$$

$$+ i_5 B\dot{L}R_{t-i} + 1_6 N\dot{D}C_{t-i} \qquad i_1, 1_3, i_4, i_6, > 0$$

$$i_2, i_5 < 0$$

(8) $\quad I_t^f = \quad$ exogenous

(9) $\quad \dot{G}_t = g_0 + g_1 \dot{T}_t + g_2 \dot{D}_t \qquad g_1, g_2, > 0$

(10) $\quad I\dot{M}_t = m_0 + m_1 PI\dot{M}_t + m_2 \dot{E}_t \qquad m_1 < 0$

$$m_2 > 0$$

(11) $\quad MS_t = \quad$ exogenous

(12) $\quad M\dot{D}_t = d_0 + d_1 \dot{Q}_t + d_2 B\dot{L}R_t + d_3 \dot{P}_t^e \quad d_1 > 0$

$$d_2 < 0$$

$$d_3 \gtrless 0$$

(13) $\quad \dot{W}_t = w_0 + w_1 \dot{P}_{t-i} \qquad w_1 > 0$

(14) $\quad PI\dot{M}_t = p_0 + p_1 X\dot{C}R_t + p_2 \dot{FP}_t \qquad p_1 > 0$

$$p_2 > 0$$

(15) $\quad \dot{T}_t = t_0 + t_1 \dot{Q}_t \qquad t_1 > 0$

The variables are defined in the Glossary of Terms.

GLOSSARY

P	=	general price index
W	=	wage rate
PIM	=	index of import prices
BLR	=	commercial bank loan rate
ED	=	excess aggregate demand
Q	=	total supply of goods and services in the national economy. Formally equivalent to GNP.

DO	=	total supply of home-produced goods and services.
EX	=	exports of goods and services
IM	=	imports of goods and services
E	=	total final demand in the national economy
C	=	total private consumption expenditures
I	=	total private investment expenditures
G	=	total government expenditures
NDC	=	net domestic credit by the banking system
MS	=	the stock of money
MD	=	the demand for money to hold
T	=	government tax and other non-capital revenues
D	=	government deficit (surplus)
P^e	=	expected prices
XCR	=	the international rate of the local currency
FP	=	index of foreign prices
Superscripts ".".	=	time rate of change of the variable; "F" foreign; "P" private domestic.

Some brief explanations of the equations are now given.

Equation (1) is the structural price determination model. It states that the rate of price change is a function of excess aggregate demand (ED), and cost push factors such as the wage rate, import prices and the price of bank credit. The lag structure is deliberately treated as indeterminate since there is no *a priori* basis for specifying particular lags for the explanatory variables.

Equation (3) is a definition of the total supply of goods and services in the national economy as the total domestic output minus that which is exported, plus the supply of foreign goods and services. The explicit identification of traded goods in the aggregate supply relation is intended to emphasise the role of imports as a safety-valve and the role of exports as a negative element in aggregate demand models of inflation in open economies. Equations (4) and (2) state the familiar final demand accounting relation and the balance equation for the final goods and services market.

The consumption function (equation 5) hypothesizes that private consumption expenditures are determined by aggregate income (Q), the commercial bank loan rate, the supply of bank credit, and the excess demand for money balances. The consumption model thus adopts a monetarist theory of expenditure determination by which, given a stable demand for money function, changes in the nominal stock of money generate changes in the level of nominal consumption expenditures; the change in nominal consumption itself being separable into changes in prices and changes in real consumption. The consumption function also adopts a finance-expenditure hypothesis. The stock of bank credit is a straightforward availability of purchasing power in advance of income variable. The bank loan rate captures two separate elements: firstly, the negative relationship between loan rates of interest and the demand for credit, and secondly, the positive relationship between bank deposit rates of interest (which are positively geared to the bank loan rate) and savings, and hence the inverse relationship between the loan rate and consumption expenditures.

The private domestic investment function (equation 7) combines the accelerator and finance hypotheses. Private domestic investment is hypothesized to respond to changes in consumption expenditures; hence the first four terms, and to changes in the availability and the price of credit. Foreign investment is assumed to be exogenously determined. This assumption does not present any problems in the present context, since we are primarily concerned with tracing the role of domestic financial variables. Government consumption and investment expenditures are treated as being influenced by the level of government fiscal revenues and by the level of the government deficit or surplus. Fiscal revenues are themselves conceptualised as a function of the level of total national supply. Import expenditures are treated as a function of the price of imports and a transaction variable, namely, the level of domestic final demand.

The demand for money function is quite conventional. It relates money demand to a transaction variable, namely GNP, interest rates, and the expected rate of price inflation. In this model, inflation imposes a cost on holders of monetary assets, while simultaneously increasing the transactions demand for money. The sign of the coefficient relating money to the expected rate of change in prices is therefore theoretically ambiguous.

Wage rates are hypothesized to be a function of lagged prices alone. This is an extremely simple function which ignores the several other influences such as profitability of the industry or firm, labour productivity, the power of labour as a class, and product market structure. We abstract from these complexities to dramatise the possible self-generating role of inflation as a consequence of wages adjusting to lagged prices. If the wage lagged price relationship is strong, then inflation possesses a self-reinforcing character.

The final structural equation to be mentioned is the import price model. It is postulated that changes in import prices are determined by changes in the exchange rate and by changes in foreign prices. This relationship being quite straightforward needs no further clarification.

Combining equations (1) to (12) and (15) and solving for $\dot{P}_t$ we derive the following reduced-form equation for price determination:

$$
\begin{aligned}
(16) \quad \dot{P}_t = A_0 \;&+ A_1 \dot{W}_{t-i} + A_2 \dot{PIM}_{t-i} + A_3 \dot{Q}_{t-i} \\
&+ A_4 \dot{Q}_{t-i-1} + A_5 B\dot{L}R_{t-i} + A_6 B\dot{L}R_{t-i-1} \\
&+ A_7 ND\dot{C}_{t-i} + A_8 ND\dot{C}_{t-i-1} + A_9 \dot{MS}_{t-i}
\end{aligned}
$$

$$+ A_{10}\ \dot{MS}_{t\text{-}i\text{-}1}\ +\ A_{11}\ \dot{DO}_t\ +\ A_{12}\ \dot{EX}_t$$

$$+\ A_{13}\ \dot{D}_t\ +\ A_{14}\ \dot{P}^e_{t\text{-}i}\ +\ A_{15}\ \dot{P}^e_{t\text{-}i\text{-}1}\ +\ A_{16}\ \dot{i}^F_t$$

Where the A_i are the combinations of the structural coefficients in equations (1) to (15).

If we substitute for PIM_t from equation (14) into (16), we obtain another reduced-form model which makes explicit the role of foreign prices and the exchange rate. Thus —

$$(17)\qquad \dot{P}_t\ =\ A_o\ +\ A_1\ \dot{W}_{t\text{-}i}\ +\ A_3\ \dot{Q}_{t\text{-}i}\ +\ .....\ +\ A_{16}\ \dot{i}_t$$

$$+\ A_{17}\ \dot{XCR}_{t\text{-}i}\ +\ A_{18}\ \dot{FP}_{t\text{-}i}$$

The self-generating character of inflation via the wage equation is seen by substituting for $W_{t\text{-}i}$ from (13) into (17) to obtain -

$$(18)\qquad \dot{P}_t\ =\ A_o\ +\ A_3\ \dot{Q}_{t\text{-}i}\ +\ .....\ +\ A_{18}\ \dot{FP}_{t\text{-}i}\ +\ A_{19}\ \dot{P}_{t\text{-}i}$$

It should be mentioned that the lagged rate of inflation can also enter the model if the adaptive expectations hypothesis is assumed to govern $\dot{P}$.

From the structure of the reduced-form equations (16) to (18) it should be apparent that many variables may enter into the inflationary process and in a complex manner for even a simple but realistic macro economic model. Since *a priori* analysis may provide little help in establishing the propulsive factors, considerable reliance has to be placed on empirical estimates of the reduced form coefficients. To this task we now turn.

EMPIRICAL RESULTS

Trinidad and Tobago

A version of equation (16) was applied to quarterly data for the period 1967 (1) to 1974(4). The assumption of static price expectations was employed so that no lagged dependent variable entered into the regression model. Furthermore, DO_t was treated as constant, and hence deleted. Supply factors are therefore partly absent from the model. The role of foreign investment was also not incorporated.

It should be noted here, that in the absence of national income data on a quarterly basis, and even on an annual basis for a large part of the period, total exports was used as a surrogate variable. In so doing, one is of course employing tacitly the export-propelled economy hypothesis. In the absence of an adequate time series on the government deficit, gross government debt was utilised as a proxy variable. The use of surrogates results in some bias in statistical estimation, but nonetheless can be shown to constitute an improvement on total omission of the missing variables. [see Wickens 11 and McCallum 6].

Regressions were conducted on log linear equations of the form:

(19) $\quad \Delta \ln P_t = B_0 + B_1 \Delta \ln W_{t-i} + B_2 \Delta \ln PIM_{t-i}$

$$+ B_3 \Delta \ln (EX/P)_{t-i} + B_4 \Delta \ln BLR_{t-i}$$

$$+ B_5 \Delta \ln NDC_{t-i} + B_6 \Delta \ln (GGD/P)_t$$

$$+ B_7 \Delta \ln MS_{t-i} + u_t$$

where u is a stochastic error term and is assumed to be normally independently distributed.

Since no prior knowledge existed with respect to appropriate lag distribution, an initial screening operation was undertaken to gain some insight into the appropriate lags and in an effort to minimise multicollinearity in the reduced-form model. The screening was conducted with the aid of stepwise multiple regression. For each explanatory variable in the model represented by equation (19), a stepwise regression was conducted with lags of up to four quarters.

The results of the exploratory regressions reveal the wage rate (lagged four quarters), the import price index lagged one quarter, the bank loan rate and the gross government debt as the primary influences on the rate of price inflation. The money supply variable appears to be quite insignificant to the explanation of quarterly price inflation in Trinidad and Tobago. Ordinary least squares were applied in a regression of $\Delta \ln P$ on the four variables identified as being significant. The following are the results:

(i) $\quad \Delta \ln P_t = 0.0074 + 0.7918 \ \Delta \ln W_{t-4} + 0.0407 \ \Delta \ln PIM_{t-1}$
$$ (3.08) \phantom{0.7918 \ \Delta \ln W_{t-4}} (2.00)$$

$$+ 0.0940 \ \Delta \ln BLR_t - 0.2987 \ \Delta \ln GGD_t$$
$$ (1.34) (-3.48)$$

$\bar{R}^2 = .6529 \qquad F = 13.88 \qquad D.W. = 1.33$

(ii) $\quad \Delta \ln P_t = 0.0065 + 0.9215 \ \Delta \ln W_{t-4} + 0.0399 \ \Delta \ln PIM_{t-1}$
$$ (3.78) \phantom{0.9215 \ \Delta \ln W_{t-4}} (1.91)$$

$$- 0.3039 \ GGD_t$$
$$ (-3.45)$$

$\bar{R}^2 = 0.6147 \qquad F = 15.89 \qquad D.W. = 1.13$

It can be seen from equations (i) and (ii) that the explanatory power of the variables is quite high. Moreover, except for the bank loan rate, the estimated regression coefficients are statistically significant at the 5 per cent level of significance. Evidently, too, the bank loan rate itself does not add much in terms of explanatory power. It is worth noting however that the estimated Durbin-Watson statistics fall within the inconclusive range for the test of autocorrelation.

Assuming for the sake of completeness that some autocorrelation might be present, we applied the Durbin two-step estimator [see Johnson 4 Chapter 8] and re-estimated equations (i) and (ii). The results presented below are less satisfactory:

(ia) $\Delta \ln P_t = 0.0107 + 0.5031 \; \Delta \ln W_{t-4} + 0.0367 \; \Delta \ln PIM_{t-1}$

$\qquad\qquad\qquad\qquad (1.48) \qquad\qquad\qquad (1.64)$

$\qquad\qquad + 0.1202 \; \Delta \ln BLR_t - 0.1873 \; \Delta \ln GGD_t$

$\qquad\qquad\quad (1.67) \qquad\qquad\qquad (-2.03)$

$\bar{R}^2 = .4097 \qquad F = 5.93 \qquad D.W. = 2.06 \qquad RHO = .3908$

(iia) $\Delta \ln P_t = 0.0143 + 0.4480 \; \Delta \ln W_{t-4} + 0.0267 \; \Delta \ln PIM_{t-1}$

$\qquad\qquad\qquad\qquad (1.82) \qquad\qquad\qquad (1.40)$

$\qquad\quad - 0.2999 \; \Delta \ln GGD_t$

$\qquad\qquad (3.09)$

$\bar{R}^2 = .4328 \qquad F = 8.12 \qquad D.W. = 2.11 \qquad RHO = .4388$

To pursue the statistical analysis of the model even further, we estimated the structural relations embodied in equations (13) and (14). Quite poor results obtained for the wage rate equation. A rather weak relationship was established between changes in the logarithms of the wage rate and changes in the logarithms of synchronous and lagged prices.

(iii) $\ln W_t = 0.1719 - 0.1674 \quad \ln P_t + 0.3408 \quad \ln P_{t-1}$

$\qquad\qquad\qquad\qquad (-1.21) \qquad\qquad (2.42)$

$\bar{R}^2 = .1220 \qquad F = 3.13 \qquad D.W. = 1.20$

The longest lag we experimented with was four quarters. It is possible that wages adjust even more slowly than we implicitly postulate to changes in the price level. More likely, perhaps, is an explanation of the poor fit in terms of the omission of variables, such as profit expectations, relative wages, and market power that many theorists suggest are important determinants. The results indicate nonetheless that whatever self-reinforcing character inflation may possess does not stem from the wage/lagged price relationship.

For the import price equation, the results were as follows. Data pertain to the period 1971(1) to 1974(4) since prior to 1971 the exchange rate was quite stable.

(iv) $\ln PIM_t = 0.0152 + 2.4166 \ln FP_t + 1.9430 \ln XCR_t$

$$(6.17) \qquad\qquad (4.00)$$

$$\bar{R}^2 = 0.7439 \quad F = 23.11 \quad D.W. = 1.77$$

(v) $\ln PIM_t = 0.00076 + 2.1109 \ln FP_t$

$$(3.82)$$

$$\bar{R}^2 = 0.4734 \quad F = 14.61$$

Evidently both foreign prices and exchange rate changes contribute importantly to the behaviour of import prices. Particularly worthy of note in the present context is the moderate push effect of exchange rate changes on the import price index and hence on inflation. This was so, despite movements in the exchange rate in both upward and downward directions. It may be argued that domestic distributors in their pricing policies respond in an asymmetric manner to changes in the exchange rate, so that while exchange rate depreciations result in higher prices, exchange rate appreciation does not correspondingly result in downward price adjustments.

Jamaica

A version of equation (16) was applied to quarterly data for Jamaica for the period 1968(1) to 1974(2). A wage series was not available, thereby occasioning the omission of the wage rate variable. Variables are measured in percentage changes to conserve degrees of freedom in the presence of negative values for some observations. The technique of stepwise multiple regressions was used in the exploratory statistical analysis. Results from the final round of ordinary least squares and the Durbin two-step estimations are presented below:-

(vi) $P_t = 0.0157 + 0.7501 \ PIM_{t-3} + 0.1488 \ BLR_{t-2}$

$$(4.73) \qquad\qquad (2.28)$$

$$\bar{R}^2 = 0.5393 \quad F = 15.73 \quad D.W. = 1.05$$

(via) $P_t = 0.0114 + 0.6745 \ PIM_{t-3} + 0.1355 \ BLR_{t-2}$

$$(3.38) \qquad\qquad (2.67)$$

$$\bar{R}^2 = 0.4208 \qquad F = 10.16 \qquad D.W. = 1.66 \quad RHO = .4514$$

(vii) $\quad P_t = 0.0084 + 0.8035 \; PIM_{t-3}$

$$(4.73)$$

$$\bar{R}^2 = 0.4574 \qquad F = 22.38 \qquad D.W. = 1.11$$

(viia) $\quad P_t = 0.0113 + 0.7169 \; PIM_{t-3}$

$$(3.20)$$

$$\bar{R}^2 = 0.2682 \qquad F = 10.22 \qquad D.W. = 1.92 \quad RHO = .4544$$

It is seen that import prices and the commercial bank loan rate are important influences on the rate of change of domestic prices. The addition of the variables net domestic credit, money supply and government deficit add little to the statistical explanation of the rate of change of prices. Thus we see that of the financial variables tested for, only the bank loan rate and the import price index appear to have any significant impact on the rate of change of prices. Furthermore, as so many commentators have argued — indeed since the 1967 devaluation and before — the rate of change of import prices is central to the inflationary process.

COMMENTARY

The statistical relationships established are not at all difficult to comprehend theoretically. When one considers the proportion of internal demand that is met by imports — of either final or intermediate products — the result for import prices seems almost so obvious as to be trivial. But one should not dismiss it too quickly. As Brewster and Thomas [3] and Thomas [10] point out, local production is geared to export markets that are in fact administered for the most part. On the other hand, local demand is satisfied by foreign production. Moreover, Jamaica and Trinidad are to all intents and purposes price-takers for imports while not being price-makers for their exports. Under these circumstances, the economies face a balance of payments constraint which prevents the use of either exchange rate appreciation or import expansion as instruments of anti-inflation policy.

In a similar vein we find the relationship of the exchange rate and the inflation rate not difficult to deal with theoretically. Several factors, namely the rigid production structure, low price elasticities of export demand, and the fact that some exporters whose output prices are quoted in foreign currency experience windfall gains in local currency, may moderate the response of exports to exchange rate depreciation. On the other hand, near monopoly power in the distribution and domestic manufacturing sectors allows cost increases resultant on devaluation to be passed on to consumers.

The relationship between the commercial bank lending rate and the rate of inflation is straightforward. One may treat interest costs as an element in the cost function. If the loan rate rises, so too should the price of the final good. Increases in loan rates of interest can therefore have an effect on the rate of inflation depending on the extent to which reliance is placed on bank credit for financing of private enterprise, and on the share of interest costs in total costs.

The push influence of wage rates on domestic retail prices has been well established statistically for Trinidad and Tobago. However, as the historical review showed, the real wage rate has actually declined over the period. One possible explanation favoured by us for these seemingly contradictory results is that the struggle conducted by labour to at least preserve its share of the national product has been met by determined and successful resistance by the owners of capital (or their representatives) to any adverse change in capital's share. While conceding increases in nominal wages, the business community has adjusted product prices in not less than equal degree. The wage inflation relationship must then be interpreted as one manifestation of social conflict between labour and capital. (For an extended discussion of this, see Bourne [2]).

CONCLUSION

In conclusion one might reiterate that the present exercise was motivated by the desire to understand the role of financial variables in the inflationary process in Jamaica and in Trinidad and Tobago. In the light of data problems and some weaknesses in econometric technique (for example the use of the static expectations assumption to circumvent the problems posed by lagged dependent variables) any conclusions arrived at from the study must be tentative; nonetheless, they do provide some insights.

We conclude that the behaviour of domestic financial variables, notably government financing, and the exchange rate have had an important bearing on the pace of inflation in Trinidad and Tobago. The monetary authorities, therefore, can endeavour to moderate the pace of inflation caused by cost-push factors such as the wage rate and foreign prices by increasing the level of government indebtedness while refraining from corresponding increases in government expenditures, and by avoiding exchange rate depreciation. The mechanism underlying the role of the government debt may be one by which an increase of the local debt withdraws purchasing power from the community and an increase in the foreign debt provides the means for closing the aggregate demand gap by increased importation.

Secondly, it can be concluded that though the availability and price of domestic bank credit are contributors to increases in the general level of prices, their separate influence has been so mild as not to warrant any grave policy concern. This is not to say, however, that explicit regulation of these variables as instruments of anti-inflation policy might not be worth pursuing.

For Jamaica, the empirical results highlight the propulsive roles of import prices and the price of bank credit. Exchange rate depreciation was too infrequent to contribute significantly to changes in the import price index over wide time spans. From the significance attached to the bank loan rate, a case can be made that the monetary authority was partly responsible for the recent upsurge in domestic prices, given the participation of the Bank of Jamaica in the determination of the loan rate.

The foregoing results and analyses raise some related and relevant issues pertaining to exchange rate, credit and foreign trade policy. Jamaica and Trinidad and Tobago are strictly speaking part of the capitalist world economy. Moreover, the links with the rest of the international economy historically, have taken the specific form of colonialism with all its implications for the former type of monetary arrangements. Domestic rates of interest move sympathetically with those in the international financial centres. Both countries are also members of the International Monetary Fund. There are therefore at least two external constraints on exchange rate policy. Firstly, there is the need to engage in defensive exchange rate shifts in response to a change in the value of the reserve currency; secondly, Caribbean economies have had to observe the rules of the game of the 'fixed' exchange rate system which existed prior to the recent 'floats' of major currencies.

In addition, there is the consideration that exchange rate appreciation may adversely affect foreign exchange earnings from visible exports and tourism with associated domestic income and employment reduction. In this case, the use of the exchange rate as an anti-inflation instrument is constrained by domestic factors.

Finally, one may want to consider what determines movement in commercial bank loan rates. It is known that commercial banks, at best tacitly and at worst as a cartel, fix these rates. The issue which remains is the ability and the willingness of the Governments to control interest rates in the pursuit of price stabilisation.

A soundly constructed anti-inflationary policy will of necessity have to consider these issues and others, such as income distribution and domestic product market structure. on which this paper did not focus. The essential concern of this paper has been to identify and measure the proximate influences of financial variables on Caribbean inflation and, as a consequence to emphasize their importance to policies of price restraint.

REFERENCES

[1]   Ally, Asgar, "Inflation – Its Effects on the Jamaican Economy", *Bank of Jamaica Bulletin*, September 1974.

[2]   Bourne, Compton, "Structure, Power and Wage Price Policy in the West Indies", *Journal of Social and Behavioral Sciences,* 20, 4, Fall 1974.

[3]   Brewster, H.R.R.: and Thomas, C.Y., *The Dynamics of West Indian Economic Integration,* Kingston. I.S.E.R., U.W.I., 1967.

[4]   Johnston, J.J., *Econometric Methods,* New York; McGraw Hill, 1972.

[5]   Latibeaudiere , Derick M., "Analysis of Inflation in Jamaica", *Bank of Jamaica Flow of Funds Division Discussion Paper,* September 1974.

[6]   McCallum, B.T., "Relative Asymptotic Bias From Errors of Omission and Measurement", *Econometrica,* 40, 4, July 1972.

[7]   Ramjeesingh, D.H., "Inflation in Trinidad and Tobago", Department of Economics, U.W.I. Mona, **(Mimeo)**, 1974.

[8]   St. Cyr, E.B.A., "Rising Prices: An Exploratory Theoretical and Empirical Study", *C.S.O., Research Papers,* No. 7, February 1974.

[9]   Thomas, Clive Y., "Inflation, Shortages, and the Working Class Interests in Guyana",University of Guyana,(Mimeo),November 1973.

[10]   ———— *Dependence and Transformation,* New York, Monthly Review Press, 1974.

[11]   Wickens, M.R., "A Note on the Use of Proxy Variables", *Econometrica,* 40, 4, July 1972.

OWEN JEFFERSON AND DARCY BOYCE

THE EFFECT OF INFLATION ON CARIBBEAN ECONOMIES

INTRODUCTION

In market economies it has become normal to expect regular, moderate increases in the price level. However, such increases have tended not to cause concern since the effects on real incomes and economic activity in general have not usually been particularly disruptive. What concerns us here, is the extraordinary large increases in prices which have occurred over the past two or three years. Such price increases have created dislocations of quite a serious order in the economies of many countries including those of the Caribbean. At the same time as the effects of this inflationary situation have been working themselves out, there have been other situations which have had some dislocating effects on the world economy. In particular, one refers to the oil crisis, the food crisis and the absence of economic growth in some of the industrialised countries. The purpose of this paper will be to examine the behaviour of certain economic and financial variables in selected Caribbean economies during the past four years in the context of the inflationary situation. In so doing, an attempt will be made to establish what effects were principally due to the inflationary conditions as well as to advance some possible explanations for the changes which occurred.

In some Caribbean countries, almost every aspect of the economy has been affected by the crisis of inflation. In some instances, of course, the effects on the same sectors have differed markedly between countries. This may imply that the effect of inflation on different Caribbean economies is a function of the difference in the economic structures. In other words, the extent and nature of economic growth and development in times of inflation may be very dependent on the main components and structural features of the economy.

Choice of Countries for Analysis

In this paper, the economies of three Caribbean countries will be examined. The three countries which will be dealt with are Barbados, Dominica, and Jamaica. Wherever readily available data allow, the analysis will attempt to cover the period since 1970 until the end of 1974. The period of analysis will therefore include that time frame within which inflation was at its fastest in the region. Like most other Caricom countries, these three countries are net importers of oil and oil products, and like all Caricom countries, they are dependent on exports (visible and/or invisible) as the main engines of economic growth. Both Barbados

and Jamaica are independent countries within Caricom and both have established their own central banks and so have more control over monetary variables
than does non-independent Dominica which is still a member of the East
Caribbean Currency Authority system. Jamaica, of course, has had more experience than Barbados in the area of central banking since the Bank of Jamaica
was established somewhat earlier than the Central Bank of Barbados.

Of the three islands, two, Barbados and Jamaica, are labelled More Developed
Countries (MDCs) while Dominica is regarded as a Less Developed Country
(LDC). In practice, however, Barbados is regarded as being at a stage somewhere
between an LDC and an MDC, though being closer to an MDC.

The paper might best present a picture of changes in the economies of the
region by looking at the economy of a MDC, an LDC, and the country which
lies somewhere between the two. Barbados is obviously this intermediate
country, and Jamaica was chosen as the MDC to analyse because of the greater
availability of economic data on Jamaica than on Guyana, and being more typical of the Caribbean economies in terms of its dependence on imports of on
than is Trinidad. Of the seven islands in the East Caribbean Common Market, all,
except Antigua, may be categorised as having agricultural bases. Dominica,
Grenada, St. Kitts, St. Lucia and St. Vincent are economies in which agriculture
contributed over 20 per cent to Gross Domestic Product at factor cost in 1971,
and in Montserrat, agriculture's contribution to GDP at factor cost in the same
year was 16.9 per cent. In Antigua, the contribution of agriculture was only 2.9
per cent. Population ranged in 1970 from 11,700 in Montserrat to 100,000 in St.
Lucia and, per capita, GDP at current market prices in 1970 ranged from EC$481
in the case of St. Vincent to EC$1,164 in the case of Montserrat. When one
examines the data for the six islands with a significant agricultural base, Dominica's population of 65,400 is midway in this range and Dominica's per capita
income is also closest to the average per capita income in these six countries.
These basic data, along with the fact that four of these six islands are Windward
islands depending heavily on the export of banana as an economic activity, seem
to point to Dominica as the best LDC Eastern Caribbean island, the analysis of
which will, more than that of any other island, portray the effects of inflation
on the Eastern Caribbean LDCs. The adequacy of the choice of Dominica to
typify the LDCs in the Eastern Caribbean is dependent, of course, on the distribution of the observations of the parameters considered (i.e. population and
per capita incomes) about the respective averages. In the case of populations,
the range is quite wide relative to the average, but with respect to per capita
incomes, there is somewhat of a cluster of values around the mean [IBRD11].

It is hoped to identify a number of effects of the inflationary situation
which have worked to promote growth in a number of sectors, to retard activity
in others, to reduce the levels of employment, to change the role of government
in the economy, to dampen investment levels and, overall, to contribute to stagnation in the economies of these countries. Possible explanations for these
phenomena will be advanced, particularly where the effects on the economies

appear to have differed somewhat from what would have been expected to occur.

The extent to which effects will be clearly identified depends on the quality and amount of data available. In some instances, the readily available data go back only to 1972; in other cases they go back to 1970 or earlier, and in other cases do not exist. A substantial amount of the analysis will, therefore, only point up situations which appear to be·subject to chan ṭe as a result of this inflationary crisis.

TREND OF PRICE INCREASES

Before the increases over time in the price indices are considered, a brief word on the cross-country analysis seems necessary. It must be made clear that in this analysis, there is no comparison of the absolute level of prices at any given time in the three countries. There will only be a comparison of the percentage rates of change in price indices in the different countries. The indices all have different base years and different weights which are shown in the Appendix. However, the base years are all in the mid-1960's and it seems reasonable to expect that the basket of goods which is representative of consumer spending in the period, 1972-1974, may well have changed from what it was when the surveys were done to determine the weights of the consumer basket. Furthermore, changes in tastes may well have been different in the respective countries, and the degree of coverage of the surveys done to establish weights will have differed significantly. In addition, the degree of subsistence production in the economy will be directly related to the accuracy of the weights in the price index as an indication of the typical mix of goods which consumers use. Changes in the price index can only be used as indicators of the changes in real incomes because of price movements and cannot, under the circumstances, be definitive of movements in purchasing power. This constraint to the use of changes in the price index must hold even more strongly when one attempts a cross-country analysis.

Over the last five years, prices have behaved somewhat differently in these countries, in so far as the trend of increases is concerned. In Barbados, for example, prices increased by 7.7 per cent in 1970 over the level of prices in 1969 and by 12.4 per cent in 1971. In 1972, prices increased by 12 per cent and an even larger increase of 21.9 per cent was recorded in 1973. An unprecedented 38.2 per cent was then recorded in 1974. Jamaica experienced much the same situation as the increase in prices in the Kingston area in 1970 was 9.7 per cent though the increase fell to 5.1 per cent in 1971. However, the rate of price increases rose again in 1972 to 9.4 per cent and was even greater in 1973 with prices increasing by 29.5 per cent. In 1974, prices increased, but by a lower percentage rate (20.8 per cent) than in 1973. In the rural areas, the increases in prices were in all these years higher than the increases in the urban area except in 1972 but the trend was the same.

The situation in Dominica was more similar to Jamaica than to Barbados in that there was a slower rate of growth of prices in 1971 than in 1970. A price increase of 12.1 per cent in 1970 was followed by only mild increases of 4.6 per cent and 3.5 per cent in 1971 and 1972, respectively. But in 1973, the percentage change in prices once more increased, this time to 12 per cent and in 1974, the increase in prices was a large 36.3 per cent. (See Table 1).

TABLE 1

% Changes in Retail Price Index 1970-74

Country		Change in Over	1970 1969	1971 1970	1972 1971	1973 1972	1974 1973
Barbados	All Items		7.7	12.4	12.0	21.9	38.2
Jamaica	Kingston Area - All Items		9.7	5.1	9.4	29.5	20.8
	Rural Area - All Items		10.5	6.8	7.7	32.1	27.4
Dominica	All Items		12.1	4.6	3.5	12.0	36.3

Note: Annual averages.

Sources: [1] 1974; [2] June 1976; [12] 1974; [10] part VII, 1973.

Some explanation may be advanced for these differences in rates of inflation. On average, the inflation rate in Barbados was higher than in the other two islands. One explanation of this might be that imported inflation was a significant factor and Barbados has a higher import component of consumption expenditure than does either Jamaica or Dominica.

Rough calculations of the ratio of total imports to Gross Domestic Product in 1970 show that Barbados' imports were equivalent to 74.8 per cent of GDP, Dominica's imports were equivalent to 66.6 per cent of GDP and Jamaica's imports were equivalent to 44.3 per cent of GDP. Other ratios were as shown in Table 2.

TABLE 2

Selected Import Ratios (%) — 1970

	Barbados	Dominica	Jamaica
Imports as % of GDP	75.1	66.6	44.3
Consumer Imports as % of GDP	33.4	30.8	12.7
Consumer Imports as % of Consumption	39.2	27.0	14.7

Sources: [11] ; [3] 1972; [2] June 1976; [12] 1973.

The average ratio of consumption to GDP over the period, 1969-1974, for Jamaica was estimated at 85 per cent and for Dominica, at 99 per cent. The figure in the Table assumes a similar ratio of 85 per cent for Barbados but even if one took 99 per cent as the ratio of consumption to GDP for Barbados the ratio of consumer imports to consumption would be 33.7 per cent and would still be higher than Dominica's or Jamaica's.

Intuitively this would seem to be the case particularly where food supplies are concerned. Both Jamaica and Dominica seem to produce far more of their food requirements than does Barbados. With world food prices rising, as a result of a tight supply situation, the effect on food prices would be much greater in Barbados than in the other two countries. In all three countries food has a weight of over 50 per cent in the overall consumer price index. In Barbados the weight was of the order of 58.7 per cent in the consumer price index with October 1965 as base; in Dominica, food and drink have a weight of 65.92 in the index with April, 1964, as base; and in Jamaica, food and drink have a weight of 47.6 in the Kingston index and 55.9 in the rural index, with January 1967 being the base for both indices. Note that a larger proportion of the Jamaican population (58.6 per cent) live in the rural areas and so, overall, food and drink must account for closer to 55 per cent than to 47 per cent in the overall price index.

It is therefore clear that an escalation of world food prices would have a proportionately greater effect in Barbados and Dominica than in Jamaica and, to the extent that Dominica imports proportionately less food than Barbados, the effects in Barbados should be stronger than in Dominica.

In terms of the consumer price index, increased costs of imported energy requirements might have had the same effect in all the islands since in Jamaica and Dominica, fuel and light have a weight of around 5 per cent in the consumer price indices and one could perhaps assume this to hold in the case of Barbados also, since the weights for household operations, etc., and transportation are similar in the indices of all three countries.[1] To add to the problem of rising prices of imports at their points of origin, freight and insurance charges have also been increasing. In Jamaica, such charges increased by 7.4 per cent in 1972, by 23.6 per cent in 1973 and by 33.2 per cent in 1974, and although such data were not readily available in the case of Barbados, it seems likely that similar increases in the cost of freight and insurance might have occurred. Dominica would most likely have suffered more than Barbados or Jamaica, because of the need for transhipment arrangements which would increase distances, handling and so freight and insurance charges.[2]

To a large extent, as well, the level of increases may have depended on the degree of price control implemented and maintained by governments. For example, in 1974 which was the major year for inflation, the rates of increase of prices for Barbados was 38.9 per cent; in Dominica, the rate of increase was 36.3 per cent; and in Jamaica, the rate of increase was 20.8 per cent in Kingston and 27.4 per cent in rural areas and, overall, around 24.5 per cent. One could, perhaps, compare the behaviour of prices in Jamaica on the one hand with the behaviour of prices in Dominica and Barbados on the other. The price control apparatus in Jamaica is much more extensive than in Barbados or Dominica, possibly because of longer experience with the implementation of such policies and the allocation of relatively more resources for the task.

It is interesting to note, though, that Barbados, which seems to have a more extensive price control machinery than does Dominica, experienced a higher rate of inflation than did Dominica. It seems, however, that prices were also rising very rapidly in Barbados in areas not normally subject to price control particularly in housing and household operations and furnishings, and furthermore, the food supply situation in Barbados seems rather more subject to imported inflation than in Dominica, and so food prices in Barbados did increase by around 40 per cent in 1974. In addition, gasolene prices, etc., increased in Barbados by almost 100 per cent because of the increase in the cost of fuel imports as well as an increased government tax on gasolene. This tax was apparently designed to reduce consumption of petrol.

So far, there has emerged some relationship between the level of inflation and other features of the economies of Jamaica, Dominica and Barbados. Specifically, it seems clear that the level of inflation has been affected by dependence of the food supply situation on foreign suppliers, the structure of consumption, the ratio of imports to GDP and the extent of price control mechanisms.

EXTERNAL SECTOR

It has been implied so far that the openness of the Caribbean countries has to a large extent been contributory to the high inflation experienced by Jamaica, Barbados and Dominica, over the last few years. A look at the behaviour of the entire external sector is necessary. Table 3 sets out the percentage growth rates of imports, exports and the visible trade deficit over the years 1970 to 1974 for Barbados, Jamaica and Dominica.

TABLE 3

Rates of Growth of Visible Trade, 1970-74 (per cent)

	Imports			Exports			Deficit in Visible Trade		
	B'dos	J'ca.	Dom.	B'dos	J'ca	Dom.	B'dos	J'ca.	Dom.
1970	15.7	20.5	26.9	6.6	16.2	-19.5	29.6	29.3	-89.0
1971	8.3	2.9	1.4	1.4	0.3	16.2	4.8	13.6	7.0
1972	11.0	9.4	8.5	5.3	5.8	1.3	13,9	9.7	13.7
1973	21.7	22.5	- 7.2	23.0	18.1	24.4	21.1	29.3	-31.8
1974	26.9	40.8	23.2	65.8	87.3	23.2	9.0	-25.3	-23.3

Sources: [4]; [2] July 1975; [12] 1974; [10] Statistical Office, Dominica.

After relatively large increases in imports in all three countries in 1970, the following year saw a decline in the rate of growth. In 1972, however, the rate of increase grew to approximately 10 per cent in all three countries. During 1973 and 1974 the rate of increase reached over 20 per cent in both Jamaica and Barbados. The explanation for this behaviour of imports is clear. The relatively good economic conditions of the late 1960s and early 1970s, together with the slow but steady rise in world prices, led to substantial increases in imports. But when the boom slackened off and incomes ceased to grow as quickly as before, the rate of growth of imports fell somewhat. In 1973, however, the prices of oil and related products increased tremendously by about 300 per cent. In addition, the lag in world food supplies behind demand led to substantial price increases. The prices of those imports into which petroleum products represent an important input also showed a sharp upward trend in 1973 and 1974, in the two countries mentioned above. For example, the prices of fertilisers in Jamaica roughly doubled in 1974 as against 1973.

The situation in Dominica, however, was somewhat different. The value of imports in 1973 fell by 7.2 per cent. This is strange in view of the generally inflationary conditions existing in that year. However, there were some factors in the situation which render a certain degree of plausibility to the occurrence. In the first place, the economy seems to have entered a phase of stagnation or even decline. Such estimates as are available [10] suggest that Gross Domestic Product increased by 14.2 per cent at current prices in 1973. However, in the context of an inflationary situation (the retail price index rose by almost 12 per cent in that year) the growth in real output (and income) could have been very small or even negative, thus depressing the demand for imports. Furthermore, the country appears to have had problems in procuring supplies of some commodities during the latter part of the year in the wake of the increase in oil prices, and the supply constraint may have been further aggravated by the country's dependence on transhipment of most of its supplies from other ports in the Caribbean.

The structure of imports has also changed since 1971, with consumer goods accounting for a smaller proportion of total imports in 1974 than in 1971. At least this has been the case for Barbados and Jamaica. Growth rates of imports by economic use are outlined below.

TABLE 4

Growth Rates (%) in Imports by Economic Use, Barbados and Jamaica

	Barbados			Jamaica		
	Consumer Goods	Raw Materials	Capital Goods	Consumer Goods	Raw Materials	Capital Goods
1972	18.7	20.5	1.8	19.0	12.1	- 7.2
1973	13.0	39.8	26.9	3.3	36.9	25.8
1974	15.6	34.9	6.4	24.6	74.6	11.0

Sources: [2] June 1976; [12] 1974.

As a result of the higher growth rates in raw materials, relative to consumer goods and capital goods, raw materials made up, in 1974, a greater percentage of the value of imports than in 1971. It is instructive to note that fuels, fertilisers, textiles, plastics, chemicals, etc., are included in raw materials. All of these items will contain a high element of oil costs and so the relatively more rapid growth in the level of raw materials may well be as a result of inflation rather than of increased production. The low growth in most selected manufactured goods and the fall in the index of industrial production in Barbados [2, June 1976] seems to substantiate the point that the rapid growth in raw material imports has been a function primarily of inflation in source countries of such raw material inputs.

From the data in Table 3, one observes that the growth in exports for the two years, 1973 and 1974, from Barbados and Jamaica was on average higher than the growth in imports. For Dominica, the growth rate of exports in 1973 exceeded that of imports but both rates were the same in 1974. This was occurring for the first time in at least five years. The principal reason for this fairly spectacular increase in the value of exports in those years was the inflationary conditions in world and commodity markets. For example, sugar began to increase in price from 1973 and so too did bananas and most of the other export crops in the region. It must be noted carefully, however, that most of the increase in exports was generally not due to an increased level of physical output but rather to the increased level of prices of these exports. There were, of course, some exceptions.

In the case of Jamaica, increases in export volumes of bauxite and alumina were recorded both in 1973 and 1974 but the volume of bananas exported in both these years fell and sugar exports fell in 1973 and, more marginally, in 1974. Rum exports also fell in 1973.

Export values increased substantially, however, in both 1973 and 1974. Increases were recorded for bauxite, alumina, bananas and sugar in 1973 and, in 1974, there were also large increases in export values of bauxite, alumina, sugar and rum.

TABLE 5

Growth Rates in Export Volumes of Selected Commodities, Jamaica (%)

	Bauxite	Alumina	Bananas	Sugar	Rum
1971	0.1	0.8	- 6.3	-2.0	44.1
1972	-7.2	17.8	0.9	-7.7	-31.0
1973	3.1	12.8	-15.3	-5.5	- 6.6
1974	8.2	16.3	-32.9	3.4	10.5

Source: [12] 1974

For Barbados, the behaviour of export volumes of the main export commodity, sugar, has been much the same as in Jamaica. Declines in sugar export volumes from Barbados were recorded in three of the four years 1971-74, with 1973 being the year of exception.

TABLE 6

Growth Rates (%) in Export Values of Selected Commodities, Jamaica

	Bauxite	Alumina	Bananas	Sugar	Rum
1971	0.1	- 6.2	- 1.1	2.3	61.7
1972	-10.0	14.9	1.2	9.8	17.5
1973	16.2	23.3	38.0	4.7	-12.8
1974	69.4	134.5	-29.8	110.4	125.8

Source: [12] 1974.

TABLE 7

Growth Rates (%) of Selected Exports, Barbados

	Sugar		Rum
	Volume	Value	Value
1971	-14.7	-10.3	-9.8
1972	-19.7	2.4	0.5
1973	12.2	19.4	19.8
1974	-11.9	60.5	55.8

Sources: [1] 1974; [2] June 1976.

Export values, however, recorded increasing rates of growth in each year since 1971 and, in 1974, sugar exports were valued at 60.5 per cent above the exports in 1973, and rum exports earned 55.8 per cent more in 1974 than in 1973.

For Dominica, much the same situation prevailed in respect of banana exports, with volumes decreasing in each of the years, 1971-1973, and increasing slightly in 1974. After falling in 1971 however, values of banana exports increased in each of the years, 1972-1974, as shown in Table 8.

TABLE 8

Changes (%) in Banana Exports from Dominica

	Volume	Value
1971	-11.2	- 1.4
1972	- 4.8	0.9
1973	-22.8	21.1
1974	11.7	33.7

Sources: [9], [10].

Very much the same pattern as exhibited in Dominica by banana exports seems to have held for banana exporting countries in the ECCM area.

It is interesting to note, however, that despite the predominance of declining production in agricultural exports in the 1971-1973 period, there seems to have been some small increases in production in 1974 and one wonders if farmers were not, in 1974, beginning to react positively to the expectations for the continuation of the unusually higher prices of 1973-1974.

Even though, therefore, exports increased substantially in both of these countries during 1973, and the percentage increase in exports was roughly of the same order as the increase in imports, the latter was on a far larger base and so the visible trade deficit would have increased.

However, the relatively faster rate of growth of exports helped to cause a decline in the pace with which the visible trade deficit was growing. Table 3 shows that between 1971 and 1973 for Barbados and Jamaica, the deficit on the visible trade was in general tending to grow at a faster rate each year. In Dominica, an 89 per cent growth in the visible trade deficit in 1970 was reduced to a 7 per cent drop in the deficit in 1971. In 1972, however, the visible trade deficit again grew, this time by 13.7 per cent and fell in 1973 by 31.8 per cent reflecting the effect of a growth rate of almost 25 per cent in the value of exports and a decline of 10 per cent in imports to which we have already referred.

Figures available for Dominica's trade balance in 1974 indicate that the rate of growth of the visible trade deficit slowed in 1974. In Barbados, because of relatively good earnings from sugar combined with import controls, the visible trade balance rose by only 9 per cent compared to an increase of 21 per cent during the previous year. In Jamaica the change was even more dramatic. An increase in the visible trade deficit of 29.3 per cent in 1973 was converted into a reduction of 25.3 per cent in 1974. Once again the reasons were good export earnings and stricter import controls.

At the beginning of this excessively inflationary period, Barbados and Jamaica and the East Caribbean Currency Authority experienced unprecedented declines in the level of their Foreign Exchange Reserves. In Barbados, Foreign Exchange Reserves at the end of 1973 were 44.5 per cent below the level of 1972. In Jamaica, the decrease was 25.7 per cent over the same period, and for ECCA, the fall was of the order of 19 per cent. For Dominica, the net foreign balance of commercial banks also fell by 54 per cent.

So great was the shock of this fall in reserves in Jamaica, that strict import rationing and control of currency movements were implemented early in 1974 and easy convertibility of the Jamaican dollar was suspended. In Barbados also, currency movements and imports were also strictly supervised and controlled by the Central Bank. In 1974, however, the Jamaican Government took advantage of the rising prices of aluminium and related products and imposed a new and higher tax structure on the foreign-owned bauxite/alumina companies operating in Jamaica. In addition, the price of sugar really spiralled in 1974 to a peak of £650 and with a larger crop of sugar reaped in 1974 than in the previous year, Jamaica's earnings of foreign exchange increased significantly. The value of exports increased by 87.3 per cent during 1974.

The effect of the high sugar prices also worked to the advantage of Barbados, for even though the sugar crop was not a particularly good one, sugar prices were so high that Barbados made record earnings for sales of sugar overseas. In addition to the usual increase in other exports, the effect of this sugar situation was to raise the value of exports for 1974 by 65.8 per cent over 1973. For Dominica, higher prices for bananas in 1974 increased export earnings in 1974 and for the ECCA region, generally, good sugar prices and a good sugar crop in St. Kitts, along with increases in the export earnings of the major export crops from this region would have helped to boost reserves in 1974. With such fortuitous circumstances prevailing in the export markets, both Barbados and Jamaica were able to raise their holdings of foreign exchange reserves in 1974. Compared with the losses in 1973, foreign exchange reserves increased by 15.4 per cent at the end of 1974 over the end of 1973 level in the case of Barbados, and for Jamaica, the increase was 73.6 per cent over the same period. Moreover, the increase in foreign exchange earnings reserves was so great that the holdings of reserves at the end of 1974 were actually 29 per cent above the level prevailing at the end of 1972. In other words, the ability of both these countries to finance the increasing volume and value of raw material imports used as inputs into manufacturing and other industries, and to finance purchases of capital goods were substantially increased in 1974 partly as a result of inflationary conditions in the export markets for their products.

During the late 1960s and very early 1970s there had tended to be a marked upward trend in the growth of income from service exports such as tourism. This factor would have tended to offset to some extent the growing deficits on visible trade. During 1973, however, there was some slowing down in the rate of growth of tourist expenditure in the countries concerned. Certainly in Dominica, there was a decline of 2.5 per cent in tourist expenditures in 1973 and in Jamaica, the increase in tourist expenditure was 7.3 per cent as compared with 18.8 per cent in 1972. The decline in the rate of growth of tourist expenditure was once again evident in Jamaica in 1974 when the increase was only 4.8 per cent. In Dominica, however, tourist expenditure increased in 1974.[3]

Total expenditure by tourists in Barbados as in Jamaica increased in 1973 but by a smaller percentage than in 1972, but in 1974 expenditure once more increased more quickly than in the preceding year.

TABLE 9

Growth Rates (%) in Tourism Arrivals and Expenditures

	Barbados		Dominica		Jamaica	
	Arrivals	**Expenditure**	**Arrivals**	**Expenditure**	**Arrivals**	**Expenditure**
1971	20.9	27.2	15.9	15.8[a]	8.1	18.0
1972	11.2	17.0	16.4	16.6[a]	7.9	18.8
1973	5.6	13.4	4.5	- 2.7	8.3	7.3
1974	3.9	14.8	8.2	13.5	8.4	4.8

Note: [a] Estimates made by authors.

Sources: Board of Tourism, Barbados; Tourist Board, Dominica; [12] 1974.

The decline in the growth rate of tourist expenditure has most certainly contributed to the slow down in the rate of growth of the positive service balance in the Balance of Payments for Barbados and the worsening in the service balance in the case of Jamaica.

TABLE 10A

Changes (%) in Selected Balance-of-Payments Items, Barbados

	1971	1972	1973	1974
Merchandise	- 9.5	-10.2	-20.1	19.4
Services	35.3	16.6	11.7	34.7
Transfers	- 5.9	6.2	11.7	42.1
Current Account Balance	12.4	- 1.7	-35.0	4.2

Source: [1] 1975.

It is also instructive to note that the increase in the rate of growth of tourist receipts by Barbados in 1974 seems connected with an increase in the services balance in 1974 over the balance in 1973. Similar data on Dominica were not available.

TABLE 10B

Changes (%) in Selected Balance-of-Payments Items, Jamaica

	1971	1972	1973	1974
Merchandise	-21.3	-11.8	-33.2	34.0
Services	8.6	96.7	-1064.7	-15.0
Transfer Payments	- 4.9	29.4	7.1	5.0
Current Account Balance	-11.9	- 6.5	-25.8	31.5

Source: [12] 1973, 1974.

The performance of tourism growth rates could well have been a result of inflation in the major countries of origin of the majority of West Indian tourists. Britain, Canada and the United States of America, all experienced double-digit or near double-digit rates of price increases during 1973 and 1974 and despite wage increases, most potential tourists from these areas might have suffered a decline in real income, particularly since there may exist a lag between price increases and compensatory money income increases. The growth in demand for tourism services in the Caribbean would therefore have suffered.

In addition, interest rates tended to rise fairly steeply in these North Atlantic countries during this inflationary period and the use of credit for travelling and vacationing would have become much less attractive than previously. This change could also have adversely affected growth rates of tourism in the Caribbean.

The effect of these changes in the structure of foreign exchange earnings is that the countries will have to monitor continuously the growth of commodity imports and promote visible exports to an even greater extent since the high growth rates in earnings from services which previously assisted to partially relieve the visible trade deficit can no longer be expected to continue. Hopefully this will induce a switch to greater emphasis on investment in the productive sectors of the economy.

Another aspect which has not yet been adequately documented is the effect of inflation on remittances from abroad. A large number of West Indian people have emigrated over time to the United States, the United Kingdom and Canada, all of which have been plagued by abnormal rates of inflation in recent times. The volume of remittances to dependents at home has built up to significant proportions in a number of Caribbean countries including those being studied here.

For example, in Jamaica, gross inflows of private transfer payments were equivalent in 1970 to 3.7 per cent of private consumption expenditure in Jamaica and moved to 4.1 per cent in 1971; 4.7 per cent in 1972 and 1973. [12, 1972, 1973, 1974]. In Dominica, gross inflows of private remittances in 1971 were equivalent to 5.4 per cent of private consumption expenditure and in 1973 had risen to 6.4 per cent [14]. Similar data are unavailable for Barbados but it seems hardly likely that the situation will be any different from Jamaica or Dominica in terms of the proportion of private transfers to private consumption. This situation indicates that until 1973 at least there was a fast growth of remittances and private transfers from abroad into some Caribbean countries and certainly that the growth rate of such transfers exceeded that of private consumption. For Jamaica, certainly, high rates of growth of the order of 27 per cent in 1971 and 36.2 per cent in 1972 were recorded in the level of gross inward private transfers though the rate of growth slowed to 14.8 per cent in 1973 and there was actually a fall in 1974 of the order of 3 per cent in the level of remittances. [12, 1972, 1973, 1974].

In Dominica, between 1971-1973, there was an increase in net remittances of the order of 42.3 per cent which represents an average annual rate of growth of 19.3 per cent for the two years. The rate of growth fell, however, in 1974 and was only 9.7 per cent.

Two factors, it would seem, were responsible for the lower growth rates (and even declines in the actual levels in Jamaica) of remittances. Both are related to inflation. It seems rational to assume that the high rates of inflation (12.5 per cent in the U.S.A., 17.5 per cent in the U.K., 10 per cent in Canada) during 1974 in the North Atlantic countries to which many West Indians have typically migrated would have reduced real incomes of West Indian migrants in those countries and such declines in income would have led to smaller increases in remittances than previously. In addition, the inflationary crisis in Britain, along with high prices for oil imports into Britain and rising interest rates in the major Western countries tended to cause a flight of capital from Britain. Britain's Government moved to prevent such drastic outflows which were seriously jeopardising the State's balance of payments, and in the process placed limitations on remittances.

The slower growth in remittances sent to dependents would have had some consequences though, perhaps, not particularly great, in the economies of these Caribbean islands. To the extent that remittances are spent locally, the growth in economic activity would have slackened and where such incomes are spent on domestic output, there could have been a depressing effect on the local economy. Of course, this is only a hypothesis which needs to be supported by more detailed research.

STRUCTURE OF CONSUMPTION

Related to the question of the significant growth of imports is that of the structure of consumption. As mentioned earlier, food prices have been among those most affected during the recent inflation. In Barbados, for example, food prices increased by 44.3 per cent during 1974 [2, June 1976]; in Dominica the increase was 31 per cent. Much of this inflation would seem to have been imported as witnessed by the 42 per cent increase in food imports into Jamaica [12,

1974] in 1974 and 24 per cent in Barbados [2, June 1976]. Local opinion has it that as a result, the consuming public has in some cases switched to greater consumption of domestically produced commodities relative to imports during 1974. In some instances, it has been reported that exports of some crops have been diverted to local consumption. This has been particularly the case with bananas, and the drastic fall in banana exports from Jamaica may lend some credence to this view. If this feature of consuming local output is going to become permanent and production grows to match the increased demand (rather than supplies simply being diverted from export markets), a contribution would have been made towards solving the problem of extreme vulnerability to external economic conditions. Apart from the rapid growth in food imports, there have been only small increases in the values of imports of other consumer goods, particularly of durable consumer goods in both Barbados [2, June 1976] and Jamaica [12, 1974]. It is to be hoped that the declining growth of imports of these products will open markets locally for domestic manufacturers.

ENERGY SEARCHES

It should be noted also that the drastic rise in oil prices has also led to renewed efforts to find new sources of energy. In Barbados the commercial production of limited quantities of crude oil has begun and output is in the region of 600 barrels per day. Substantial resources of natural gas have also been located. In Jamaica, there has been renewed interest in the search for oil both on- and off-shore, and Dominica is also anxious to explore new possibilities of thermal energy which might exist in the main volcanic sections of the island. Already Britain has spent considerable amounts in exploring geothermal energy sources in Dominica. One effect therefore of inflation (particularly of imported energy prices) has been to provide the necessary incentive for increased investment in energy exploration enterprises. The prospects of using solar energy have also become brighter and, in Barbados, the production and installation of solar water heaters has become more widespread.

INVESTMENT

Traditional theory postulates that inflation should encourage investment. The basis of this assumption is that inflation tends to increase the profit margins of producers and distributors and so induce increased investment. Furthermore, if the producer expects inflation to continue he should try to avoid increased costs of investment which would occur if he postpones the decision to invest.

This does not appear to have been the situation in the Caribbean countries examined. While the level of investment measured in current prices increased in some countries during this recent inflationary period, the increases seem to have been due principally to the higher price level for capital goods.

Furthermore, there appears to have been a tendency for the public sector to increase its share of investment relative to the private sector.

In Jamaica, for example, the government has been actively engaged in land development for farming, road construction and housing development on a larger scale than usual. Similarly, in Barbados and Dominica a relatively high proportion of the investment activity in recent years has been in infrastructural works carried out by the public sector.

A number of hypotheses can be put forward as to why actual behaviour of private investors in the Caribbean does not conform with what the theory would lead us to expect. The first one is that even if inflation in the region actually gives rise to increased profits, the structure of ownerships of assets is such that increased investment in the private sector is not necessarily made. Most of the profitable concerns in many countries are foreign owned and their profits tend to be repatriated rather than reinvested or saved locally. For example, investment income flows out of Jamaica grew by more than 20 per cent during 1974. [12, 1974]. The second reason is that even when businesses are locally owned, the propensity to invest, generally speaking, tends not to be high. Profits which have been made in the distribution sector or in traditional export industries such as sugar tend not to be channelled into new production areas. Of course, to the extent that governments by way of taxation can appropriate some of these surpluses, as in the case of Jamaica and Barbados, through bauxite and sugar levies, respectively, investment in the public sector may be increased. But investment in the public sector tends still to be heavily weighted towards infrastructure rather than directly productive activities. And in many cases recurrent expenditure has been pressing so hard on recurrent revenue that governments have had to increase their levels of borrowing quite substantially so as to carry out such investment as was undertaken by the public sector.

Inflation in the United Kingdom has been one factor making for the substantial depreciation of the exchange rate of the pound in international money markets. Other things being equal, the depreciation of the value of the pound should have served to encourage North American investment in the area. But as mentioned earlier, there were many other factors working in the opposite direction. Not least of these, was the decline in demand in the North American market for the type of export commodities particularly the output of enclave industries for which investment funds have usually been made available by private investors.

PUBLIC SECTOR ACTIVITY

As pointed out earlier, some governments have been tending to play a much more important role as far as capital expenditures are concerned. In Jamaica, for example, government capital expenditure during 1974 increased by 77.1 per cent over the previous year. Even allowing for rising prices this represented a substantial increase in real investment as far as the public sector was concerned. This was made possible partly by the relatively large increase in revenues as a result of the new tax structure imposed on the bauxite/alumina industry. It may be possible that the introduction of these new tax measures were to some extent triggered by the effect of external inflation. Such inflation, in the absence of additional foreign exchange yielded by the tax on the bauxite/alumina companies, could have caused considerable dislocation in Jamaica's economy, as it did in late 1973 where foreign exchange reserves declined dramatically.

TABLE 11

Growth (%) in Government Activity, 1970-1974

	Current Revenue			Current Expenditure			Capital Expenditure		
Year	B'dos	J'ca	Dom.	B'dos	J'ca	Dom.	B'dos.	J'ca.	Dom.
1970	19.6	22.0	15.8	18.5	22.6	23.1	19.6	30.4	158.3
1971	13.5	14.8	16.2	6.2	15.9	16.3	13.6	22.4	34.0
1972	8.4	14.9	-5.2	26.7	26.2	-0.6	0.4	17.8	136.1
1973	16.2	22.3	3.5	37.4	26.9	33.8	23.6	16.0	-71.1
1974	17.5	47.6	-3.1	26.0	47.9	-9.5	37.2	77.1	-40.3

Sources: [5]; [12] 1974; [10] part VII; [7] 1971-74; Dominica Ministry of Finance; [13].

The large increases in capital expenditure which were made by the Barbados and Jamaica governments were paralleled by similarly large increases in current expenditure for 1973 and 1974. Even by 1972, the rate of growth of the current expenditure of the Jamaica government had reached 26 per cent and this rate of growth increased significantly in 1974 to almost 48 per cent. In Barbados, for the period, 1970-1972, the average annual increases in current expenditure were around 12.6 per cent. (See Table 3). However, in 1973, the increase in current expenditure was of the order of 37.4 per cent and in 1974 the increase was 26 per cent. Certainly in the case of Barbados, in 1974, stringent controls were instituted over current expenditure so that all expenditure which was not particularly urgent was omitted and the control of expenditure even went so far as to the point where there was a curtailment of the creation of new positions within the public sector. Government's role as one of the primary generators of employment was therefore substantially affected by the high rate of inflation. With fewer possibilities of employment in the government sector the onus was therefore thrown onto the private sector to absorb a far larger percentage of the increase in the labour force than was customary. With relatively new investment in the private sector and some firms actually reducing their labour force, there has been very little additional job creation in the private sector and so the unemployment problem in the country would seem to have worsened.

In Jamaica, the unemployment situation would hardly have shown much improvement during the recent inflationary phase. However, this was not because of government curtailment of employment expansion but rather as a result of the slowing down of investment in the private sector. For example, a relatively high percentage of new housing investment during the period since mid-1973 was undertaken by the government [12, 1974]. In addition, the government's 'crash programme' to relieve unemployment (financed out of the additional revenues occasioned by the bauxite levy) helped to create a substantial amount of employment. However, with the increase of the labour force and the slowing down of the rate of expansion of the private sector, the result might merely be to prevent the rate of unemployment from increasing.

Data available for Dominica suggest that public sector activity declined drastically in 1973 and 1974 after having been at very high levels during the preceding three years. Capital expenditure in the public sector actually fell by 71.1 per cent and 40.3 per cent in 1973 and 1974 respectively. In the latter year government current expenditure also fell by 9.5 per cent. These declines reflected the behaviour of government revenue which in turn arose out of the low level of economic activity in the economy. With the declining profitability of the banana industry and the slow growth of private investment in other activities there has been little real growth, if any, in the economy over the past few years. Government revenues actually declined by 5.2 per cent in 1972 and increased by only 3.5 per cent in 1973. In 1974, current revenue declined by 3.1 per cent. With inflation proceeding at a brisk pace and in the absence of budgetary aid, large cuts had to be made in certain items of current expenditure so as to more nearly achieve some sort of balance in the budget.

As far as capital expenditure is concerned, the main sources would be external borrowing. As indicated above, there was no surplus in the current account to be applied toward the capital budget. Furthermore, the rigidity of the currency board system, under which countries like Dominica operate, places severe limits on the extent to which investment can be financed locally. Specifically, one refers to the requirement for the very high sterling backing of currency issued by the East Caribbean Currency Authority and the consequent diminution of ECCA resources available for investment in the member territories of the ECCA.

External aid to Dominica appears to have declined absolutely in 1974. We have been unable to identify the reasons for this phenomenon though one could possibly advance the view that Britain's own domestic economy was not particularly buoyant in 1973 or 1974 and this could have affected British aid overseas. As far as external borrowing is concerned, the main source for the less developed countries of the region has been the Caribbean Development Bank. However, disbursements of funds from the CDB up to the end of 1974 were low in relation to loan approvals (disbursements were only 8.4 per cent of approvals), reflecting the normal lags experienced by institutions of this nature and accentuated by the high proportion of loan approvals accounted for by projects with long gestation periods such as ports. In addition to the normal delays associated with the implementation of projects, the problem was compounded by the inability of many governments of the less developed countries to find the counterpart funds necessary for project implementation. Furthermore, in an inflationary situation delays in the implementation of projects can mean large increases in costs resulting in the need for applications for additional loans if the project is to go forward. In the case of Dominica, for example, inflation during 1974 caused an increase of the order of 34.1 per cent in the value of loans for projects approved before the end of 1973[6, 1974]. It should be noted that the Government of Trinidad and Tobago, the only Caricom country which was in a position to benefit from the rapid escalation of oil prices, has provided a fund of TT$10 million in the Caribbean Development Bank to assist the less developed countries to meet their counterpart requirements. This has already begun to assist in the speedier implementation of projects.

The significant increase in public sector capital expenditure in Jamaica and Barbados which was referred to earlier was accompanied by significant increases in the public debt since recurrent expenditure tended to rise at a faster rate than recurrent revenue, and so tended to reduce the contribution of current account revenue surpluses in financing capital expenditure. The level of public borrowing in gross terms in Jamaica during 1974 was more than 60 per cent [12, 1974] higher than in the previous year and, in Barbados [2, June 1976], the public debt outstanding at the end of 1974 was approximately 36.7 per cent over the level at the end of 1973. Note that in both these countries the increases in 1974 represented larger increases than in 1973 of the order of 40 per cent. The rapid rate of growth of public borrowing in relation to recurrent revenue is almost sure to lead to a situation where an increasing share of the latter will have to be directed towards servicing of the public debt. Already for Barbados, debt service has been growing during 1971-1973 at over 36 per cent per annum as compared with an annual average of 12.6 per cent for current revenue. In Jamaica [12, 1974] debt service payments increased by about 30 per cent in both 1973-4 and 1974-5, a rate of growth which was tending to outstrip the increase in recurrent revenue. Percentage increases in debt service in Dominica [7, 1971, 1975, 1976] were also outstripping the growth in current revenues from as early as 1970.

It should be noted, however, that the sizeable increase in public borrowing tended to be accompanied in Barbados by a noticeable increase in the share obtained from local sources. In Barbados, domestic debt accounted for 69.2 per cent of the total national debt in 1972 but by 1974, had increased this proportion to 76.3 per cent. This shift towards greater dependence on the local capital market might have been due in part to a conscious effort on the part of governments to reduce the burden of future foreign debt service payments, particularly in the light of increased uncertainty about future foreign exchange earnings. A number of other factors might have influenced the decision. Among these one can point to the sharp increases in interest rates abroad and the reluctance of many institutional investors overseas to lend at reasonable rates on a long term basis at a time of instability in the international money markets.

Domestic money markets could hardly escape some effects of the international monetary situation together with the heavy increases in local borrowing by governments. If the Treasury Bill rate is taken as a rough indication, one finds that in Barbados, for example, the rates increased sharply from somewhere under 6 per cent at the end of 1972 to 8 per cent at the end of 1973. Approximately the same rate was prevailing at the end of 1974. A similar trend was also noticeable in Jamaica when the rate moved from approximately 5 per cent to more than 7 per cent and in Dominica, the rate moved from 8.1 per cent at December 1974. The inflationary situation appears therefore to have affected the cost of government borrowing both at home and abroad but in terms of availability of funds the local markets seemed to offer a distinct advantage especially with the tighter controls imposed in all three states on outflows of funds for investment purposes.

TABLE 12

Movements (%) in Government Treasury Bill Rates

Year Ended	Barbados	Jamaica	Dominica
1970	7.10	4.38	n/a
1971	6.69	3.52	6.65
1972	5.98	4.97	5.70
1973	8.10	7.14	8.10
1974	8.04	7.20	9.53

Note: n/a — not available

Sources: [2] July 1975; [9].

GROWTH OF OUTPUT

Although data at constant prices are not generally available, such crude indicators as exist, suggest that the relatively high rates of growth of domestic output which occurred in many countries during the late 1960s and early 1970s did not continue into the period of abnormally high inflation. In Jamaica, for example, national income at current prices increased by 10.9 per cent in 1971, 22.2 per cent in 1972, 15.4 per cent in 1973 and 32.0 per cent in 1974. The percentage increases in prices during these years (see Table 2) tend to indicate, however, that while there was some real growth in national income between 1970-1972, 1973 and 1974 might have been years of zero growth — and even decline in income. It is, however, appreciated that the consumer price index is not a suitable deflator for national income at current prices but in the absence of any other index, use of the consumer price index does provide a little guidance as to the movements in real income.

It may be postulated that increases in real output should occur during inflationary conditions since the increased level of prices, and correspondingly of profits, should encourage producers to invest and produce more.

As the phenomenon of 'stagflation' (inflation accompanied by stagnating output levels) has clearly demonstrated, this proposition is not necessarily valid depending as it does on the doubtful assumption that as a general rule, consumer prices can be increased at a faster rate than costs of production without at some point affecting the level of sales. It also assumes that profits are, as a matter of course, reinvested in the production sectors. For the Caribbean, this hypothesis may well not be confirmed.

It might now be useful to examine briefly some trends in the main productive sectors of the economy.

Agriculture

The inflationary period has resulted in increases in prices of agricultural produce both for export and domestic consumption during the years 1973-74, (See Tables 5,6,7,8) spectacular increases being recorded in the prices of some commodities such as sugar during 1974.

Other things being equal, such price increases should have acted as a spur to increase production. It is as yet too early to make authoritative statements about whether this is the case since it is the 1975 crop rather than the 1974 one which will reflect such an increase, but it is clear that the cost structure has also been rising thus making inroads into the surpluses generated by higher prices. The costs of sugar production[4] in Barbados, for example, have increased by 19.1 per cent in 1972, by 0.3 per cent in 1973 and by 33.4 per cent in 1974. The following increases in prices of selected fertilisers in Jamaica during 1974 also illustrate the point.

TABLE 13

Prices of Selected Fertilisers in Jamaica

	J$ Per ton		Percentage Change
	1973	1974	
Urea	133.6	323.8	142.4
Complex 12-24-12	127.4	241.7	89.7
Super Triple Phosphate	134.5	252.1	87.4
Sulphate of Ammonia	77.9	178.6	129.3
Muriate of Potash	95.0	114.9	20.9

Source: [12] 1974.

In addition, the price of machinery, fuel, transportation, etc., rose very considerably during the same period. Wage rates have also been rising in agriculture. Wages in the agricultural sector in Barbados, for example, rose by 40 per cent in 1974. Wage increases tended to originate in the export sector, where in some cases windfalls were being experienced, and permeated through to the domestic sector of agriculture. Wages in the sugar industry in Barbados are normally set very early in the calendar year and out-of-crop wages which apply also to non-sugar agriculture are usually tied to sugar wages.

With all these inputs rising in price, the cost structure of agriculture in the region rose significantly and it is not clear whether the inflation has increased the overall profitability of the sector. As far as some crops are concerned, costs might even have risen faster than prices, thus reducing profitability.

In some instances, as in the case of sugar, governments have taxed away significant portions of the windfall gains arising from spiralling prices. But it is not always the case that such funds are channelled back into the agricultural sector. The inflationary situation has also increased the price of agricultural land, thus making land acquisition more difficult especially for the small farmer. Thus at a time when food prices are rising abroad and the supply situation is also tight, it is not clear that the necessary conditions have yet been created for bringing about the spectacular increases in food production which the circumstances warrant.

Construction

The indications are that the rate of construction of new housing at all levels has tended to stagnate during the inflationary phase. In Jamaica, most construction activity was undertaken by government and in the case of housing, the number of houses started remained around the 1973 level. In Dominica, building permissions also remained around the same number as in 1973 and in Barbados, applications for building permits, reported building starts and quarrying production, all declined in 1974. This is not surprising in view of the combination of higher building costs, increased interest rates on mortgages reaching 14 per cent in Barbados [12, 1974; 1, 1974; 8], and rising land prices at a time when the population is also faced with spiralling costs of other basic necessities such as food.

It might be argued that if rates of inflation are high and are expected to continue, the rational approach is to borrow now since the burden of repayment will be progressively reduced as inflation proceeds. However, this approach ignores the downpayment which has to be made in respect of mortgages and in a period of rapid inflation, this may be increasingly difficult to come by.

The decline in the private sector activity in this sector has been partially offset by public sector activity financed by loans from international agencies or by windfall revenues derived from export commodities such as sugar or bauxite.

There has also been some slowing down in expansion of hotel accommodation because of a levelling off of the rate of growth of the demand for such accommodation. In Jamaica, in particular, hotel construction had been a significant portion of activity in the sector during the late 1960s and early 1970s.

Another very important area of construction is that of road building and repair. The period under review witnessed sharp increases in the cost of both materials and labour associated with this activity. With limited government revenue available, particularly in the case of Barbados and Dominica, much of the new road construction programme had to be shelved temporarily and even road repair had to be cut back in the attempt to keep public expenditure within reasonable bounds.

The result of the circumstances outlined above has been a tendency towards reduction of the employment generated by the construction sector. Traditionally this sector has been a relatively large employer of both skilled and unskilled labour. As a consequence the pace of expansion of the sector has important implications for movements in the overall level of employment.

Manufacturing

The relatively slow rate of growth of real income and employment appears to have led to a reduction in the growth of demand for manufactured goods. In addition, because the sector depends heavily on imported inputs, it has felt the effects of increases in costs of raw materials and freight rates.

As far as the enclave industries are concerned, the high rate of inflation in the Caribbean countries relative to North America tended to erode some of the cost differential which made location in the Caribbean advantageous in the first instance. This factor together with sagging demand as a result of recession in the United States led to closure or retrenchment of labour in some of these industries in Barbados and Jamaica.

In terms of the level of output in this sector, the index of industrial production in Barbados fell in 1974 and in both Dominica and Jamaica [1, 1974; 12, 1974] there were declines in output of a number of manufactured goods.

Tourism

'Stagnation' in the traditional tourist markets tended to reduce the amount of discretionary income available for expenditure on foreign travel. Furthermore, air fares tended to increase and so has the cost of hotel accommodation in the Caribbean. Rising interest rates in many of the major tourist markets would have made borrowing for travel and vacationing more expensive and much less attractive than previously and this factor would also have helped to reduce the growth rate of tourist arrivals. In the context too of expectations of continuing price increases for basic necessities, potential consumers of tourist services might have been inclined to adopt a 'cautious' approach to luxury spending in tourism. It is perhaps because of these reasons that the rate of growth of tourist arrivals has fallen in Barbados and levelled off in Jamaica. (See Table 9).

The reportedly high and increasing cost of hotel accommodation in the Caribbean, particularly in Barbados and Jamaica, seems likely to have severely reduced the competitive position of the tourist industry in these countries and unless this decline in competitiveness can be averted, the trends evident in 1973 and 1974 are likely to be accentuated in future years.

Already the effect on employment of the depressed state of the industry has been quite apparent resulting in hotel closures and retrenchment of staff. The situation is most serious in Jamaica where over-expansion of capacity in the late 1960s and early 1970s, together with the recent reduction in demand, led to a dramatic plunge in occupancy rates leading to many closures.

As far as this industry is concerned, one limited benefit may be gained from the recent inflation. The high cost of imported foodstuffs together with some shortages of supply should induce some marginal switch towards locally produced commodities. But unless the agricultural sector can respond by increasing production quickly to the desired level, even this limited benefit may disappear.

INCOME DISTRIBUTION

The data available for Caribbean countries are grossly inadequate for the purpose of measuring short period changes in income distribution. As a consequence it is almost impossible to assess the impact of inflationary pressures on relative income changes as between different segments of society.

Evidence drawn from the experience of other countries suggests that redistribution of income in favour of property owners is one of the more pervasive effects of rapid inflation. It would be surprising if this were not the case in the typical Caribbean country and in the case of Jamaica, employed labour seems to have received a smaller share of national income in 1974 than it did in 1973, since labour income was 59.2 per cent of total factor incomes in 1974 and 63.2 per cent in 1972 [12, 1974].

This information seems to lend some support to the hypothesis that in times of inflation, incomes are skewed in favour of property owners.

It must be remembered, however, that rates of increase of income can be vastly different between different groups of wage and salary earners. It is difficult to generalise on this point but it would seem rational to suggest that in a period of inflation those workers who are able to protect their real incomes most vigorously are precisely those who, on average, are few and in great demand and so started off close to the top of the income pyramid. In such a case, the distribution of income could have become more uneven.

Within recent months Jamaica, at least, has begun to attempt to formulate a strategy aimed at correcting this situation by providing guidelines for wage and salary movements involving higher percentage increases at the lower than at the higher level. But it remains to be seen whether this laudable policy can be enforced outside the narrow confines of the public sector.

CONCLUSION

This survey, focussing as it does on a few aspects of a limited number of countries, has covered only a small proportion of the many effects which inflation has had on Caribbean economies recently. However, even from this limited evidence, it is clear that the recent inflationary period has served to highlight the known structural weaknesses of Caribbean economies and their very heavy dependence on the rest of the world.

The initial impact of the imported inflation was on the balance of payments. Traditional deficits on current account were worsened by the escalating prices of oil, food and a variety of other goods and services. Favourable movements in the price of sugar on the world market helped some countries to recover a portion of the huge loss of reserves and in Jamaica increased taxes on the bauxite/ alumina sector also helped to partially retrieve the situation.

In Dominica, as elsewhere, imported inflation manifested itself in a rapid rise in consumer prices and a tendency towards a creation of deficits (or widening of already existing ones) on government current accounts. With limited means of credit creation and the absence of sufficient quantities of aid the country was forced to restrict government expenditure quite sharply thus reinforcing a tendency towards stagnation of the economy.

Increased prices of imports affected the cost structure of all sectors adversely. In some sectors, real output was reduced and in other sectors where demand was growing the traditional bottlenecks, especially in agriculture, prevented output from responding sufficiently quickly to benefit from the favourable situation.

Typically the rate of growth of real income and employment tended to be relatively low. This was accompanied by a situation in which it appears tentatively that the income distribution tended to worsen as those at the bottom of the income scale were least able to protect themselves from the ravages of inflation.

The recent international situation has provided convincing evidence of the dangers of excessive reliance on external sources, especially for basic supplies such as food. It has pinpointed other areas where greater self-reliance can be a reality. One can say, then, that although economic growth may have been retarded in the short-run, real development could be enhanced in the future if the challenges provided by recent events are squarely faced.

APPENDIX

Weight of Different Items in Consumer Price Indices

Barbados

October 1965 = 100

Item	Weight
Food and Beverages	58.7
Housing	9.1
Household Operations and Furnishings	8.9
Clothing	6.9
Medical and Personal Care	5.3
Transportation	5.5
Education and Miscellaneous	9.8
All Items	100.0

Dominica

April 1964 = 100

Food	65.2
Alcoholic Beverages and Tobacco	8.3
Housing	8.9
Household and Miscellaneous Items	4.6
Fuel and Light	5.4
Clothing and Footwear	9.5
Services	6.4
All Items	100.0

Jamaica

January 1967 = 100

	Kingston	Rural
Food and Drink	47.55	55.91
Fuels and Household Supplies	3.82	5.27
Housing	12.36	4.55
Household Furnishing and Furniture	3.83	7.41
Clothing and Accessories	8.81	13.29
Personal Expenses	9.77	7.00
Transportation	3.22	3.73
Miscellaneous	10.64	2.84
All Items	100.00	100.00

FOOTNOTES

1. Weights obtained from [2] June 1976; [12] 1974; and from data supplied by the Statistical Department, Dominica.

2. Data on freight and insurance in Jamaica's case from [12] 1973, 1974.

3. Dominica Tourist Board.

4. Data supplied by Barbados Sugar Producers Association.

REFERENCES

[1] Barbados, Central Bank, *Annual Reports.*

[2] —————— , *Economic and Financial Statistics.*

[3] —————— , Economic Planning Unit, *Economic Surveys.*

[4] —————— , Statistical Service, *Annual Overseas Trade Report.*

[5] —————— , Ministry of Finance and Planning, *Estimates of Revenue and Expenditure,* 1976-77.

[6] Caribbean Development Bank, *Annual Reports.*

[7] Dominica, Government of, *Estimates of Revenue and Expenditure.*

[8] —————— , Government of, Central Housing and Planning Authority.

[9] Eastern Caribbean Currency Area, *Annual Report and Statement of Accounts for Year ended March 31, 1975.*

[10] ECLA, *Economic Activity – Caribbean Countries,* 1973, 1974.

[11] International Bank for Reconstruction and Development, *Caribbean Regional Study,* Volume II, 1975.

[12] Jamaica, National Planning Agency, *Economic and Social Surveys.*

[13] —————— , *Statistical Yearbook,* 1973.

[14] Mulk, Ikhatiar Ul, *National Accounts of Dominica with Supporting Economic Accounts of the Institutional Sectors for 1971 and 1973,* Government of Grenada.

WILFRED L. WHITTINGHAM

INFLATION IN THE CARIBBEAN COMMUNITY AND LATIN AMERICA

The paper considers briefly some methodological aspects of measures of inflation then goes on to look at general inflationary trends, making some comparisons with Continental Latin America and the Caribbean Community Area.
Finally, there is a short section on anti-inflationary policies with emphasis on
the Caricom Area.[1]

CONCEPT AND MEASUREMENT OF INFLATION

Inflation may be said to exist when the flow of purchasing power in a community exceeds the flow of goods and services and manifests itself in rises in the
general level of prices. This definition implies that an adequate measure must
concern itself with the relationships between changes in values and quantities or
changes in prices. The kind of measure required should be comprehensive in
scope covering the range of goods and services including interest and rent.

Indexes commonly used to measure overall measurements in prices include
comprehensive indexes of producer's prices relating to domestic supply of commodities and of consumer prices. The latter are the well known consumer price
indexes or retail price indexes. The implicit GDP or GNP deflator which is
essentially the ratios of constant price magnitudes to the current price magnitudes is another particular indicator of overall price movements. The constant
price series makes considerable use of a wide range of price statistics in converting values to a common unit and measurement.

Since the study of inflation would include not only the levels and changes in
overall prices over a period of time, but also the manner in which prices in various sectors, industries, etc. and of different commodities and services are be-
having relative to each other, a number of different price statistics are indicated.
That is to say, it is necessary to identify the precise sources of price increases and
the relative impact exerted by each source. Series of prices of imports, if possible
classified according to kind of commodity, are also very necessary in studying
inflation, especially in countries which can be classified as 'open economies'.

Most of the comprehensive price statistics mentioned above as necessary for
measurement and analysis of inflationary conditions are not generally collected
on a regular basis in the Caricom area countries. For Jamaica, however, an impli-

cit GDP price deflator series has been published for a number of years at least
up to 1973. (The current validity of this deflator is not known but there have
been indications that at least some of the individual price parameters and
assumptions need revision).

In addition there are the consumer price indexes and indexes of retail prices
which are available for most of the Caricom countries. The problems with these
indexes are:

Outdatedness or lack of currency: For the most part the indexes (up to
1974) are based on weighting patterns derived from household expenditure
surveys carried out many years ago when incomes, consumption patterns and
tastes and the type and quality of goods available were different from what they
are now. For example, the Guyana survey was conducted in 1965; Trinidad-
Tobago survey between December 1957 and June 1958; Barbados survey relates
to observations in 1960/61 and 1964; Jamaica between July 1963 and May
1964. New indexes for Guyana and Jamaica based on more recent household
survey information beginning 1974 have been published recently.

Lack of comprehensiveness: The indexes are not as comprehensive as would
be desired for a broad measure of inflation. A large number of individual commodities and services such as interest, insurance and some personal services are
excluded from some of the indexes. For example, in the series relating to the
countries mentioned above, the Barbados index covers 134 items, Guyana's
241 items, Jamaica 207 items, Trinidad-Tobago 274 items. Moreover, the indexes are limited to the lower income segment of the population. (The newer
indexes mentioned above for Jamaica and Guyana have been broadened to include consumption patterns of persons with higher levels of income than previously included.) In addition the Laspeyres formula of fixed base-weighted
averages which is widely utilized in calculating price indexes in the Caribbean
and many other countries has a built-in rigidity which precludes addition of new
items.

Difficulty of Comparisons: Inter-country comparisons of rates of inflation
become somewhat difficult because of the differences in scope, coverage,
weights-base periods etc. of the indexes.

Despite all these limitations the consumer price index remains the single
most widely used measure of inflation in the Caribbean and elsewhere.

Another important influence on inflation which might not be sufficiently
covered in these indexes relates to tourism, especially in those smaller countries
where tourism constitutes a relatively large sector. Tourism expenditure in these
cases would tend to represent a significant amount of purchasing power of
people with higher incomes and taste preferences bidding for available supplies
of local goods and services.

Looking at inflation in the broad sense implied by the definition in paragraph
one indicates that it would be useful to compare the real level of output GNP or
GDP in constant prices with some measure of the stock of purchasing power in

monetary terms. Indicators of purchasing power include money supply, loans and credit outstanding. The lack of constant price GDP data in the Caribbean countries has already been mentioned. Money supply and commercial bank loans data are widely available but data on credit extended are less readily available. Even so, it appears that a significant part of liquidity in the Caribbean may be outside the control of the established financial institutions so that measures of the stock of purchasing power would tend to be understated.

INFLATIONARY TRENDS

It is redundant to say that the present inflation is a world-wide crisis. The internationalization aspects, especially in terms of duration, have taken on an ominous character which gives rise to gloomy predictions of world-wide economic and social disaster. Fortunately, there are indications that the worst may be over since during 1975 there have been indications of reduced rates of inflation in some of the developed countries and indeed also in some developing countries. Of course, the recent increase in petroleum prices from October 1975 will influence upward the trend of the price indexes for the next few months, as the higher prices get reflected in prices of commodities and services further along the production chain.

Table 1 gives increases in consumer price indexes for selected countries from 1965 to 1974. The first point of interest is that, everywhere with the exception of Argentina and Uruguay, the 1974 price increases were higher than in the earlier years. Also, with few exceptions, the rates of increases for the more developed countries have been lower than the rates for developed countries. It is curious that the rates of increase for Guatemala, Honduras, Venezuela and Iran are so low. The reasons may have to do with the methodological aspects of the indexes but this point need not occupy us too much at this time. Curiously, however, in all cases except Guatemala the weights-base period is of fairly recent origin and the number of individual items on which prices are collected are roughly the same or larger than the number of items included in the indexes of the Caricom MDCs. The Guatemala series covers only 47 items and relates to a survey of households dating back to 1946.

The price increases for Caricom countries during 1974 are among the highest of all countries listed in the table. Interestingly the index for Guyana shows lower growth rates since 1965 than for all other Caricom countries. In the Bahamas the Consumer Price Index increased by 13 per cent closer to the lower rate of increase experienced by developed countries of the world and lower even than the Guyana rate. The lower increases for Guyana can be explained partly by the outdatedness of the consumer expenditure pattern on which it is based, i.e., the year 1956. Another partial explanation is the fact that the index measures only the spending patterns of lower income groups in two urban centres. Explanation of trends in the Bahamas index for 1974 is not possible from available information. However, the Bahamas C.P.I. has a recent weights-base period and is broad in terms of both number of price series and the range of

TABLE 1
ANNUAL RATES OF GROWTH OF CONSUMER PRICE INDEX
OF SELECTED COUNTRIES

Countries	1965–1970	1972	1973	1974
Italy	3.0	5.7	10.8	19.1
Japan	5.5	4.8	11.7	24.5
United Kingdom	4.6	7.1	9.2	16.0
United States	4.3	3.3	6.2	11.0
West Germany	2.4	5.5	6.9	7.0
Argentina	19.3	57.8	61.5	24.2
Bolivia	5.9	6.5	31.6	62.9
Brazil	29.0	16.7	10.9	24.9
Colombia	10.0	14.3	22.8	24.4
Costa Rica	2.5	4.7	15.2	30.1
Dominican Republic	1.2	7.9	15.1	13.2
Ecuador	4.7	7.9	13.0	23.4
Guatemala	1.5	0.6	13.8	16.0
Honduras	1.7	3.7	6.0	12.6
Mexico	3.5	5.0	11.3	32.8
Uruguay	59.9	76.5	97.0	77.2
Venezuela	..	3.0	3.9	8.5
Ghana	3.4	13.5	10.2	27.7
India	6.8	5.8	17.4	28.8
Iran	1.4	6.5	9.8	14.0
Bahamas	7.0	n.a.	n.a.	13.1
Barbados	6.5	11.8	16.9	38.9
Dominica	6.2	3.5	12.0	36.3
Grenada	6.9	n.a.	n.a.	n.a.
Guyana	3.1	4.5	8.9	17.5
Jamaica	5.9	5.9	19.2	27.2
St. Kitts-Nevis-Anguilla	7.1	6.3	4.2	28.4
St. Lucia	5.7	7.9	13.4	34.2
St. Vincent	n.a.	2.6	16.3	35.5
Trinidad and Tobago	4.6	9.3	14.8	22.0

n.a. = not available

Source: Caricom Countries – on basis of Official Statistics; Other countries [ECLA 7; UN 10].

the income levels of households covered in the primary survey.

It is observed that the Food sub-group indexes in Caricom countries have grown faster than the overall indexes. Examination of price indexes for a large number of developed countries, in general, show the opposite pattern during 1974, for example, Belgium, Denmark, the Federal Republic of Germany, but not the U.K. and Japan. It would appear that in general, countries more dependent on imports of foodstuffs tended to experience higher rates of increase in the food index relative to the total index. In Argentina, 'a developing country' which produces a large part of its own foodstuffs, the Food index grew significantly slower than the total index in 1974.

Openness of the Caribbean economies, so frequently a 'whipping boy' in discussing economic problems, also comes in for its share of castigation for inflationary conditions. This fact is also of importance in the general Latin American context.

One publication [7 Vol. 1] characterized the openness as 'internationalization of rising prices', pointing out that the motive force is located in the industrialized or 'central economies' and is then transmitted to the 'peripheral countries'. We support this view as pertaining also to Caricom countries, but maintain a reservation that internal motive force does exist to some degree in the countries of this Area if only in the lack of sufficient effort to channel domestic consumption into local foodstuffs which can be produced and substituted for some imported goods.

Table 2 shows one measure of the degree of openness for selected Latin American and Caricom countries. The coefficients of openness in Latin American countries are relatively low compared with some European countries and much lower than for all Caricom countries and Bahamas. The higher ratios in Costa Rica come somewhat closer to the Caricom rates, but it must be pointed out that Caricom rates may be somewhat over-stated because GDP at factor cost is used rather than GNP at market prices. One curious relationship is the very low coefficient of openness for Uruguay which has one of the highest rates of inflation. A major part of the explanation for the high Uruguay inflation would seem to lie in the severe currency depreciation which has occurred in the free market rate of the Uruguayan peso vis-à-vis the U.S. dollar; to the extent of more than 400 per cent[1] [2 and 10] between the end of 1971 and 1974. Depreciation against other major world currencies obviously would also have occurred.

With the major exception of Uruguay and Chile most other Latin American countries have had only moderate or no devaluation of their official exchange rates in recent years. In the Caricom countries, with the exception of Jamaica, mild currency depreciation resulted from the link with the Pound Sterling during 1974. During 1975, however, the rate of depreciation increased further and helped induce Barbados and Guyana to sever their links with Sterling and establish fixed rates with the U.S. dollar. Jamaica had taken a similar step in 1973.

TABLE 2

RATIOS OF EXTERNAL TRADE[1] TO GROSS NATIONAL PRODUCT IN CURRENT PRICES FOR SELECTED COUNTRIES

Country	1960-62	1973	1974P
CARICOM COUNTRIES[2]			
Barbados	51.0	51.5	55.7
Guyana	50.0	57.2	66.7
Jamaica	29.4	30.4	36.5
Trinidad and Tobago	59.5	31.5	40.6
LATIN AMERICAN COUNTRIES			
Bolivia	20.2	29.7	n.a.
Brazil	7.7	8.9	n.a.
Colombia	14.5	14.2	n.a.
Costa Rica	24.1	34.2	n.a.
Ecuador	18.3	24.1	n.a.
Uruguay	14.0[3]	13.6	n.a.
DEVELOPED COUNTRIES			
U.S.A.	3.4	5.5	7.5
U.K.	19.2	19.7	24.3
Japan	8.3	9.2	n.a.
Federal Republic of Germany	15.0	17.3	20.5

P   = Provisional
n.a. = Not available
1   Average of imports and exports.
2   GDP data used in place of GNP except for Jamaica.
3   1961-1962

Source: Latin American Countries – IMF *International Financial Statistics* quoted in ECLA [7 part 1 Vol. 1]; Caricom Countries [8], [11], [12].

TABLE 3

INTERNATIONAL RESERVES IN SELECTED COUNTRIES
(Millions of US Dollars, at the end of each period)

Country	1970	1973	1974	Percentage variation 1973-1972	Percentage variation 1974-1973
Bolivia	45.5	72.1	190.5	20.8	164.2
Brazil	1,187.0	6,417.0	5,252.0	53.4	18.2
Colombia	206.0	534.0	449.0	64.3	-15.9
Costa Rica	16.3	42.4	38.1	7.7	10.1
Ecuador	83.0	241.0	350.0	68.5	45.2
Uruguay	175.0	232.0	217.0	17.2	6.5
Barbados	16.6	26.0	26.5	20.5	1.9
Guyana	20.4	14.0	n.a.	-62.0	n.a.
Jamaica	139.2	127.4	190.4	-20.2	49.5
Trinidad and Tobago	43.0	47.0	390.3	-19.4	730.4

Source: IMF [2]

The recent Latin American experience with the monetary variables — levels of international reserves, money supply, domestic credit etc. — shows that these have not all moved together in the same direction. Generally, levels of reserves were down in 1974 except notably for Bolivia, Ecuador and Venezuela. Money supply increased substantially between 1973 and 1974 in some countries, and so did domestic credit. Caution is indicated, however, in imputing a one-to-one relationship between increased money supply and the rise in prices in Latin America since weaker relationships are observed for some countries.

TABLE 4

LATIN AMERICA AND THE CARIBBEAN: COMPARISON BETWEEN INCREASES IN THE MONEY SUPPLY AND IN THE CONSUMER PRICE INDEX IN SELECTED COUNTRIES

	1972	1973	1974
Bolivia			
Increase in money supply	25.2	34.3	43.4
Increase in consumer price index	6.5	31.6	62.9

(continued)

Table 4 *contd.*

	1972	1973	1974
Brazil			
Increase in money supply	38.9	48.0	34.8
Increase in consumer price index	16.7	12.9	27.2
Colombia			
Increase in money supply	27.1	30.7	9.5
Increase in consumer price index	14.3	22.8	24.4
Costa Rica			
Increase in money supply	14.2	24.1	6.3 (9)
Increase in consumer price index	4.7	15.2	26.0 (6)
Ecuador			
Increase in money supply	21.6	30.7	36.5
Increase in consumer price index	7.9	13.0	23.2
Uruguay			
Increase in money supply	52.1	74.5	62.2 (12)
Increase in consumer price index	76.5	97.0	107.3 (12)
Barbados			
Increase in money supply	8.6	8.1	17.0
Increase in consumer price index	11.8	16.9	38.9
Guyana			
Increase in money supply	22.7	14.5	31.3
Increase in consumer price index	4.5	8.9	17.5
Jamaica			
Increase in money supply	7.8	20.5	18.8
Increase in consumer price index	5.9	19.2	27.2
Trinidad and Tobago			
Increase in money supply	22.6	7.6	34.0
Increase in consumer price index	9.3	14.8	22.0

Note: The figures in brackets are the number of months considered in relation to December 1973.

Source: ECLA [7 part 1 Vol. 1]: [2].

This situation is not unlike the general Caricom pattern where large changes in the level of 'liquidity' in 1974 are accompanied by large changes in the level of retail prices. The Barbados case, however, is notable, in that whereas during 1974 when expansion of several indicators of liquidity taken together[2] was smaller than in 1973, the rises in prices were much greater.

The Uruguayan inflation since 1972 resulted also from the breakdown of stabilization policies in effect between 1968-1971 and the conscious policy of bringing national prices especially of foodstuffs into line with international prices. That is to say, inflation was tolerated to assist in improving the relative position of agriculture. The earlier policy of protection of local industry through import control was also modified after 1971.

This extreme example of Uruguay is certainly different for the general approach seems to be to restrict the imported inflation elements as much as possible while attempting to manipulate the internal elements so as not to restrict growth in output.

If there is a lesson to be learnt from the Uruguay situation, it is probably the following: even where the coefficient of openness is low unchecked currency depreciation combined with large increases in the money supply and reduced protection to domestic industry against foreign imports will combine to produce significant levels of inflation.

ANTI-INFLATIONARY POLICY

The current worldwide inflation is a new economic phenomenon in terms of its pervasiveness. Exceptions, of course, have to be made for several Latin American countries, but nearly all of these, at least since the 1960s, have reduced their levels of inflation (measured in terms of retail price indexes) to relatively tolerable levels. Consequently, the understanding of the current complex worldwide inflation is very difficult and one author concedes that it has become necessary to devise policy solutions before understanding the primary causes of inflation. [See Perry 4].

The major anti-inflation strategies expounded or practised are well known and include: income and price controls; fiscal policy — varying the levels of taxation and spending; control over the levels of liquidity, exchange rate and use of import controls. Various combinations of some or all of these are grouped under headings such as Keynesian, Monetarist or Structuralist. What is important, however, is whether a particular strategy or technique is effective in a particular situation. In passing, it may be worth noting one conclusion from a study covering the entire postwar period that "when controls (prices and incomes) were in force (in the UK) there was no general tendency for the inflation (retail prices) to come down". [Parkin 3].

In general, the measures pursued in the Caricom region during 1974 included: tightening of price controls; import restrictions; promoting development of agriculture and manufacturing: fuel conservation; money and credit controls;

fiscal policy measures including granting of subsidies and restrained government spending; foreign exchange control; and moral suasion. Except for fuel conservation the other activities are not new, but there was increased emphasis on tightening of controls and broadening of the scope of these activities.

The range of goods under price control was substantially widened and existing control measures were more vigorously enforced. Prices of staple food items and basic raw materials were particularly singled out for control. In Jamaica, for example, Government engaged itself in distribution of foodstuffs through special outlets at subsidized prices. In an effort to curb imported inflation varying forms of import restrictions have been instituted. For example, in Guyana, practically all imports have been brought under a system of licence and non-essential imports were restricted. Jamaica and Trinidad and Tobago, too, widened their system of import licencing. At the beginning of 1974, in Jamaica a ceiling on the value of total imports was implemented though mainly as a foreign exchange conservation measure. There were also continued efforts to seek out sources of lowest prices for imports including Third World and non-traditional trading partner countries.

Activities aimed at increasing production were also intensively pursued. Central banks in some countries collaborated with commercial banks in pursuing policies geared at limiting imports particularly of durable consumer goods, as well as redirecting funds to more productive domestic activities. In Barbados, for example, the commercial banks restricted consumer credit, and at the same time, made credit facilities available for export and for development of tourism and agriculture. Some increases in agriculture output during 1974 are traceable to these measures. In Guyana, incentives were given to farmers who increased their acreage of certain crops, while in Jamaica the emphasis on increased production seemed to have been on domestic food consumption. In this respect, the 'Operation Grow' programme has met with some measure of success both in terms of output and substitution of some imported food items.

Governments increased the number of goods subsidised as well as the level of subsidy to producers and consumers. Some of the consumer items receiving subsidies during 1974 were fertilizers, rice, flour, dairy products and fuel. In Trinidad and Tobago, the price of fuel to the consuming public remained at the 1973 level as the Government bore the increase in price. In Jamaica, the Government established a fuel subsidy scheme (equivalent to the rate of increase in electricity rates) for all consumers of electricity. It should also be noted that although the region's fuel import bill rose substantially during 1974 as compared with 1973, the growth would have been much higher were it not for some measure of fuel conservation imposed by governments.

Although aggregate government expenditure for the region increased during 1974, expenditure on non-productive activity was restrained. In most countries, particularly in Jamaica and Guyana, some planned development projects had to be postponed and others considerably reduced in scale. In Barbados, the Government curtailed the recruitment of staff. Because of such anti-inflationary measures, aggregated government budget deficit for the area declined from approximately EC$623 million in 1973 to $489 million in 1974.

It should also be mentioned that the question of moral suasion formed an integral part of the anti-inflationary measure during 1974. It was considered important to develop a greater sense of resourcefulness among the population.

SOME CONCLUSIONS

Because the high rate of inflation in the Caricom region is a relatively recent phenomenon, experience with anti-inflationary measures is very limited. It would seem, therefore, that it is necessary to draw on all possible sources in developing policies that can be effective in an inter-dependent world economy to minimise the impact of inflation.

The eclectic approach may not be very successful, however, because of structural and other differences between other economies and those of the Caricom Area. In addition, the high degree of openness and dependence on the outside world with respect to both consumption and production, which has been mentioned above, would also indicate need for a different approach. Moreover, the measures utilized in many other countries have not been markedly successful as indicated above, but obviously some lessons can be learnt. Most importantly, it must be remembered that the overriding priority is to increase output and employment.

The strategy necessary to minimise inflation must be comprehensive in scope, for no single approach seems capable of producing the desired result. Anti-inflationary measures should aim at reducing external influence on local prices in addition to regulating and monitoring local factors which influence price increases.

First of all, we focus on the imported aspects. The most important element is the purchasing of goods in the cheapest markets. These attempts should be supplemented by bulk purchasing of commodities such as is being done in Jamaica, or purchasing of commodities through a central agency as done in Guyana by the External Trade Bureau. The experience of these two countries should be shared with the rest of the region. Another important element is the exchange rate structure. The experience of some Latin American countries[3] and common sense would suggest that it is important to avoid currency depreciation since import prices are directly increased, and higher export earnings induce increases in domestic prices of goods and services. Selected import controls must also be used in an attempt to influence consumption patterns away from imported goods to domestic goods, thereby inducing increased production. The problem here is to ensure that an adequate supply of goods are available and indicates the necessity for complementary efforts to stimulate domestic production.

Secondly we turn to the internal factors. These are several, of which the most important revolves around increasing output of goods and services; in other words, attempting to increase the right side of equation $MV = PT$. Despite some progress much more needs to be done to increase output and provide goods at internationally comparable prices.

The services sector which has been generally neglected in favour of manufacturing should be promoted with equal vigour. Here shipping, marine insurance, advertising and distribution are important sub-sectors. The first two have direct implications for import costs as well. The problems with the distributive sector include, *inter alia*, too many middle men which means unnecessary mark-up at several levels in the distribution chain. Here also the experience of the Guyana External Trade Bureau may be useful to the rest of the region. Government's participation in the distribution sector could help circumvent artificial shortages caused by hoarding of goods. There is also need for greater supervision at all levels of production in both the private and public sectors to improve productivity levels.

The next category of internal measures may be lumped together, that is monetary and fiscal measures. These two have external or imported elements, namely, exchange rates, international commodity prices, foreign reserves, etc. Problems with this sector relate to the fact that there is still a large non-monetary sector in the countries of the Caricom Area. In most countries also, the fiscal resources and tax revenue base is very limited. Moreover, the LDCs of the area have little scope for utilizing monetary policy in the absence of a Central Bank. The only comment here is that perhaps as time passes the expertise in choosing the appropriate 'mix' of techniques and applying them correctly will improve.

Another category of measures is incomes and price control. There is a long history of price control and indirect control of incomes in the sense of redistribution through taxation measures. However, not much if anything has been done to limit increases in income in the same way as price increases have been controlled. It should be remembered that income controls in some other countries have been less than successful and certainly have not been pursued for any length of time. The main problem seems to be political rather than technical, that is, is there a community will to make such measures work in our present free enterprise system? Despite the history of other countries, it appears that it is now necessary to introduce some control over increases in income.

A final category of measures relates to influencing tastes and consumption patterns. Obviously these would affect both external and internal factors in the inflation process. It is clear though that foreign consumption patterns normally require foreign goods or imitative domestic production despite high prices. The measures would therefore have to aim at re-education and strong influencing of consumption pattern through incentives, import restrictions etc. Guyana has perhaps moved furthest in the use of these measures compared with other Caricom countries, and it will be recalled that the rate of growth of the Consumer Price Index in Guyana is lowest in the Caricom Area.

It would seem that all the weapons are in the economic armory but the technique of using them selectively and in the right combinations needs to be developed.

FOOTNOTES

1. The views expressed in this paper are those of the author and are not necessarily shared by the United Nations Economic Commission for Latin America, Office for the Caribbean, to which organization he is attached as a staff member.
2. That is, money supply, instalment credit and commercial banks loans and advances. See Economic and Financial Statistics, Central Bank of Barbados.
3. The cost of living of Uruguay, for example, rose 40 per cent during a seven month period of 1963 following two and a half years of relative stability of both prices and the exchange rates. The exchange rate, however, had been under pressure in 1963, and a 50 per cent devaluation preceded the sharp price rises. See [6].

REFERENCES

1. Bank of Jamaica, *Bulletin,* September 1974, Vol. XIII, No. 3, Jamaica.
2. International Monetary Fund, *International Financial Statistics,* July 1975.
3. Parkin, Michael, "Where is Britain's Inflation Going", *Lloyds Bank Review,* July 1975, No. 117, Lloyd's Bank, London.
4. Perry, George L., "Understanding World Inflation", Papers and Proceedings of the Eighty-seventh Annual Meeting of the American Economic Association in *The American Economic Review,* May 1975.
5. The Royal Economic Society, *The Economic Journal,* June 1973, Vol. 83, No. 330; London.
6. United Nations, Economic Commission for Latin America, *Economic Survey of Latin America,* 1964.
7. ———————— , *Economic Survey of Latin America,* 1974, Part I, Vols. I and II.
8. ———————— , Economic Commission for Latin America, Office for the Caribbean — *Economic Activity, Caribbean Community Countries,* 1974 (ECLA/POS 75/4).
9. ———————— , Statistical Division, *Statistics of Prices and Quantities and National Accounting in Constant Prices — A System of price and quantity statistics,* (E/CN. 3/427, 14 August 1972)
10. ———————— , *Monthly Bulletin of Statistics,* August 1975.
11. ———————— , *Yearbook of National Accounts Statistics, 1969;* New York.
12. ———————— , *Yearbook of International Trade Statistics,* 1972-1973; New York.

WILLIAM C. ALLEN

INFLATION IN THE BAHAMAS[1]

BACKGROUND

The Bahamas has essentially a services economy, with service sectors accounting for slightly more than 70 per cent of GDP and non-service sectors accounting for under 30 per cent. Tourism dominates the service sectors as the spillover effect of tourism permeates the entire economy. Directly or indirectly, tourism is estimated to determine over 55 per cent of GDP, and to supply 60 per cent of the foreign exchange requirements.

The main non-service sectors are construction, agriculture and mining. During the 1960s construction accounted for about half of the non-services total, and was itself geared mostly to tourist related facilities.

The economy of the Bahamas is an extremely open one. Exports of goods and non-factor services approximate 70 per cent of GDP, and imports of goods and non-factor services are about 60 per cent of GDP. Given this openness, the economy is greatly affected by external factors, one of the most important of which in recent times has been the very high level of inflation.

Because of the predominance of goods from the United States in the Bahamas external trade, price inflation in this major trading partner works its way quite quickly through the local economy, resulting in a high degree of imported inflation in the Bahamas.

Monetarily, the Bahamas is also linked to the United States. Since February 1973, the Bahamian dollar has been pegged at par to the United States dollar. Although the policy of The Central Bank is to sell or purchase Bahamian dollars against either the United States dollar or the Pound Sterling, the volume of foreign currency transactions of the system is overwhelmingly in United States dollars while the demand on the Central Bank for sterling is considerably smaller.

The net effect of all this has meant that *ceteris paribus* the economy of the Bahamas is exposed to a great many exogenous variables lessening, to some extent, the impact of domestic policy measures.

THE EXPERIENCE

In 1969, at the end of the boom period the annual rate of inflation in the Bahamas was about 10.6 per cent. This followed a period of fairly rapid growth in wages due to the increased demand for labour and the relatively inelastic local supply of it. During this period the country was in a state of over-employment, with many people holding two jobs. This was coupled with significant expansion in the money supply brought about by an increase in consumption as well as capital outlay. There is a weakness in the data compiled in this period but they suggest that the inflation was of both a demand pull and cost-push origin. Thereafter, from 1970 to 1972, there followed a period of moderate inflation, little growth in the money supply and a fall-off in employment.

TABLE 1 — RETAIL PRICES

(Percentage annual change)

	1969	1970	1971	1972	1973	1974
All Items						
Period average	8.9	6.1	4.6	6.8	5.5	13.0
End of period	10.6	4.6	5.3	5.8	9.4	13.6
Components (Period Average)						
Food	4.7	4.7	4.8	7.4	5.6	18.4
Housing	12.7	7.7	5.5	8.1	3.2	8.4
Clothing	3.5	0.4	3.6	10.0	5.5	11.9
Transport	2.8	1.4	1.4	4.7	5.2	15.5
Other	10.0	9.4	4.7	4.1	8.0	11.5

In 1973, as a result of the worldwide commodity price increases which began in the latter part of 1970, and increases in the cost of fuel, prices overall rose significantly. The retail price index which showed an increase of 5.8 per cent in 1972, ended 1973 with a 9.4 per cent increase. Traditionally, price increases in the Bahamas fall somewhere between the increases in the United States and the United Kingdom, its major trading partners. The 9.4 per cent increase in 1973 compared with 8.5 per cent in the United States and 10.3 per cent in the United Kingdom.

In 1974, there was a distinct acceleration in the rate of price changes, beginning in the first quarter. The effect of the four-fold increase in fuel prices had begun to work its way through the economy. Increases in the transportation component of the retail price index jumped from 5.5 per cent posted at the end of 1973 to an average annual increase of 13.5 per cent for the first three months of 1974. It was never to fall below this for the remainder of the year.

By far the greatest contributor to the price increases of 1974 was food, which in the first quarter was averaging an annual increase of 16.8 per cent. In the second quarter, led by phenomenal increases in the price of sugar, the food component, with a weight of 34.3 per cent, was increasing at an average rate of 20.5 per cent. By the third quarter a deceleration of the increase in food had

TABLE 2 - ANNUAL RATES OF RETAIL PRICE INCREASES. 1974

	Weight	Year to Month End											
		Jan.	Feb.	March	April	May	June	July	August	Sept.	Oct.	Nov.	Dec.
Food	343	+16.81	+16.78	+16.74	+19.32	+21.13	+21.42	+20.51	+19.95	+17.66	+17.48	+18.81	+18.35
Housing	350	+ 7.26	+ 7.15	+ 6.81	+ 7.37	+ 7.66	+ 6.94	+ 7.48	+ 7.81	+ 8.25	+10.63	+ 9.70	+ 8.39
Clothing and Footwear	101	+10.60	+14.23	+11.66	+10.80	+12.86	+13.97	+12.48	+13.85	+13.61	+12.50	+11.48	+11.93
Transport	91	+13.07	+12.63	+14.92	+16.32	+14.25	+13.61	+13.62	+14.48	+13.48	+15.08	+16.24	+15.45
Health and Personal Care	70	+ 7.00	+ 6.01	+ 6.10	+ 8.19	+ 7.67	+ 7.52	+ 7.97	+ 7.24	+ 9.17	+ 8.75	+ 8.28	+ 8.08
Recreation and Reading	44	+11.40	+16.81	+14.41	+11.50	+ 2.09	+ 4.31	+ 4.55	+ 6.161	+12.60	+14.25	+13.94	+15.57
Other Goods and Services	101	+12.49	+10.22	+10.63	+12.52	+ 9.15	+ 7.99	+ 8.15	+ 9.56	+10.33	+13.00	+14.04	+12.11
All Items	1000	+12.08	+12.29	+12.07	+13.18	+13.15	+13.13	+12.93	+13.25	+12.92	+13.82	+14.23	+13.57

been achieved; nevertheless, the average annual increase in the fourth quarter of 1974 was about 18.2 per cent.

The categories 'Housing' and 'Health and Personal Care' posted the smallest increases for the year, and further research indicates that changes in these areas were tempered by a fall-off in demand. In the case of housing this is underscored by an apparent excess supply.

For the year, the overall increase in prices was 13.6 per cent — 1.4 percentage points higher than the United States, but considerably below the 19.1 per cent increase in the United Kingdom. In 1974 roughly 70 per cent of total commodities was purchased from the United States, while less than 20 per cent came from the United Kingdom.

In 1974, evidence shows that the inflation was essentially of the cost-push variety, and totally imported. The narrow money supply was fairly stagnant throughout the year, and all categories of commercial bank credit were down except for building and construction which showed only a modest gain of less than one million dollars.

Inflation was the most dominant single economic problem facing the country and the government in 1974, and was given the highest priority in terms of policy decisions. Acknowledging that the source of the inflation was essentially beyond the control of local authorities it was nevertheless consciously felt that efforts should be aimed at avoiding a demand-pull effect on the situation. On 1 February, in consequence of this, and as a result of external pressures as well, the prime rate was raised from 9 per cent to 9½ per cent. Average fixed deposit rates followed this increase, rising by roughly 0.5 per cent.

There was no need to adopt a specific policy with respect to the Balance of Payments. The higher import prices had a self correcting influence and in real terms — non-oil imports fell for the year while non-oil exports showed a significant gain. The visible trade gap (oil not included) narrowed from a deficit of $182.8 million in 1973 to $167.1 million.

By the end of the second quarter of 1974 after very heavy increases in certain 'bread-basket' items, particularly sugar, it became clear that a more direct policy had to be adopted. It was explicitly acknowledged that: a) stopping inflation was beyond our control; b) the element of price that could be effectively controlled was the profit margin; and c) it was necessary to eliminate the notion that any and all increases in the price level would be accommodated by the authorities.

On 6 August 1974 the Prices Commission took certain steps which included placing the price of bread and milk under control, and amending the regulations to eliminate the practice by merchants of evading price control through the importation of unlisted brands. The result was that food prices fell from the annual increase of 19.9 per cent posted in August to 17.7 per cent in September. The cost of milk fell by as much as 15 per cent and the cost of bread fell as much as 20 per cent.

The initial shock of these measures had very positive results.

TABLE 3 — MONEY SUPPLY

End of Period	Currency in Active Circulation	Demand Deposits	Narrow Money Supply	Savings Deposits	Fixed Deposits	Foreign Currency Deposits	Broad Money Supply
1973							
December	19,935	54,908	74,843	45,445	51,813	142,090	314,191
1974							
January	18,614	56,130	74,744	45,826	49,347	131,363	301,280
February	18,831	55,752	74,583	46,945	52,376	142,456	316,360
March	20,410	54,645	75,055	48,026	54,874	171,905	349,860
April	18,957	55,888	74,845	48,728	55,898	159,017	338,488
May	20,806	58,080	78,886	48,167	57,244	198,425	373,722
June	20,288	58,180	78,468	48,025	58,454	188,850	373,797
July	19,101	57,219	76,320	47,732	61,321	187,887	371,260
August	20,365	57,515	77,880	48,295	62,622	133,203	322,000
September	18,739	54,312	73,051	47,981	67,002	271,960	459,994
October	18,235	54,043	72,278	48,438	66,911	234,101	421,728
November	20,097	56,122	76,219	46,967	66,668	223,554	413,409
December	19,195	57,348	76,543	45,544	68,835	208,488	399,410

Source: The 1974 Annual Report of The Central Bank of The Bahamas.

WAGES

During the late 1960s, the limited data available suggest that wages were rising at an annual average of around 15 per cent, well in excess of the cost-of-living increases. These wage increases were generated by the relatively inelastic supply of local labour coupled with the expanding demand resulting from the stepped-up economic activity at this time. Unions were generally weak during this period.

Following the economic slow-down which began in 1970 wage increases became more moderate. The last broad salary review of the public sector took place in 1970 when salary increases ranged as high as 20 per cent. Constraints on the government's budget did not allow for a major review until 1975, although two cost-of-living adjustments were allowed — one being in July 1973 of $26 per month and another in July 1974 of $20 per month.

As a result of government holding the line on public sector wages, there was a reduction in real terms of wages in 1974.

Although the unions had become somewhat stronger, wage settlements in 1974 were quite moderate. In February, hotel workers negotiated an increase of 14 per cent spread over the two-year term of the contract.

There was no need to adopt an incomes policy. In fact it was acknowledged that there was no internally generated inflation in 1974. This is supported by monetary data and the Balance of Payments performance.

Money supply data revealed that while there was little change in transactions balances, fixed deposits increased from $51.8 million at the end of 1973 to $68.8 million at the end of December 1974. During the year loans and advances to the private sector decreased by $18.2 million, and there was a significant run-down of inventories. There was an increase in net international reserves of $6.5 million.

The cash reserves of the banking system continued at roughly twice the required reserves, as in 1973, and the Central Bank foreign reserves stood at year-end 1974 slightly higher than the balance at the end of 1973.

CONCLUSION

Because of the slump in economic activity, and the extreme openness of the Bahamian economy, inflation was in fact imported. There was little that could be done about this and concentration was essentially on influencing the expectations of the public regarding inflation.

The mechanism was set up through the Prices Commission to ensure that profit margins were not overly expanded and wages were kept virtually unchanged. In retrospect, the year was not as bad as was generally expected, and even the fuel increases were absorbed without the disruption that was generally feared.

FOOTNOTE

1.   Analysis based on retail prices only.

GLORIA FRANCIS

PRICE TRENDS IN BARBADOS, 1968-1973

INTRODUCTION

Persistent price increases have been a widespread phenomenon since the late 1950s, with most of the developed countries experiencing rates of price increase around five per cent annually up to the mid 1960s. Thereafter a general steep rise in world commodity prices raised inflation rates in industrialized economies to between eight and ten per cent per year.

Barbados, a small, open developing economy which depends almost totally on imports from industrialized countries to satisfy consumption needs, has been particularly vulnerable to these external influences, and has been registering cost-of-living increases of over eight per cent per annum since 1968. This rate is considerably higher than that experienced in the three other more developed economies (MDCs) of the Caricom region — Guyana, Jamaica and Trinidad and Tobago — which display rates of 2.8 per cent, 7.0 per cent and 5.2 per cent respectively for the same period.

Several factors could partially explain this. Firstly, Barbados is unique among the MDCs in that almost its total arable acreage has, for most of its history, been under sugar cane cultivation for export to the neglect of other agriculture. Prices for its export sugar are 'protected' by preferential treatment through the Commonwealth Sugar Agreement and its negotiated price quotas, and therefore remain more or less stable over time. As a result, farmers are reluctant to diversify into crops with higher degrees of risk and uncertainty with regard to yields and income. The lack of emphasis on domestic non-sugar agriculture is therefore more marked than elsewhere in the region and a very large proportion of the food requirements of the country must be supplied by imports from metropolitan countries. There are other internal factors which can contribute to the price increases which the country has been recently experiencing. These include the oligopolistic nature of the distribution sector and certain direct import taxes.

This paper examines the extent to which prices of imports (that is, the combined cost — insurance-and-freight (c.i.f.) prices of goods imported into the country) influenced retail prices in Barbados during the period 1968-1973. The analysis centres around a comparison of the trends displayed by an index of import prices compiled for this purpose, with those of the retail price index compiled by the Barbados Statistical Service. The import price index was disaggregated by category of good along lines similar to those of the retail price index in order to allow this comparison.

We first deal with the contribution of each component of the c.i.f. price — the external factors — to the overall increase in import prices; then we look at other factors — the internal variables — which influence the prices of goods and services to the final consumer. Factors examined include frequency of changes and level of import tariffs, consumption taxes and other levies and distributors' margins and other commercial practices.

We also attempt to relate the level of prices of goods and services within the economy with the freight on board prices of exports. We look at the extent to which imported inputs are used in production and at domestic price levels during the period to obtain an idea of the costs of production and their comparability with export prices. We also compare trends in import and export prices for an indication of the direction of the country's terms of trade.

COMPARATIVE MOVEMENTS IN IMPORT AND RETAIL PRICES

Since the present index of retail prices for Barbados was compiled, it has recorded a relentless upward movement of monthly consumer prices, with a marked absence of fluctuations between months or of seasonal variation within individual years. Retail prices increased at a steady average annual rate of 8.2 per cent during the period 1968-1973. The actual increase between years grew from five per cent (December 1968-December 1969) to approximately 17 per cent (December 1972 -December 1973).

The index for import prices shows an annual growth rate of six per cent during the years 1968 and 1973. Increases in this case, however, grew from 1.2 per cent between 1968 and 1969 to approximately nine per cent between 1972 and 1973. A comparison of the growth rates for import and retail prices by commodity groupings (Table 1) indicates that in all cases retail prices are influenced to a large extent both by external and by internal factors.

FACTORS INFLUENCING IMPORT PRICES

The import price of a commodity is here defined as the f.o.b. cost of the commodity at source, plus the insurance and freight charges imposed on the importer. Thus, import prices reflect changes in these three components — the external variables which are outside the influence of the domestic economy.

World export prices rose at an average rate of 6.9 per cent for the period between 1963 and 1973, while the prices of raw materials and manufactures show rates of 6.3 per cent and 4.6 per cent respectively. Minerals and petroleum both show a price increase of 6.1 per cent for the period.

Export prices offered by Barbados' main trading partners — U.K., U S.A. and Canada — display growth rates of 5.1 per cent, 5.0 per cent and 5.9 per cent respectively for the period 1968-1973. In all instances the pace of increase quickened dramatically during the years 1971 to 1973.

TABLE 1

COMPARATIVE GROWTH RATES FOR IMPORT AND RETAIL PRICES 1968-1973

(Percentage)

	Import	Retail
All Items	6.0	8.2
Food and Beverages	5.8	8.8
Household Op. and Furnishings	4.5	5.8
Medical and Personal Care	1.0	7.2
Clothing	6.6	7.4
Transportation	12.7	7.1
Housing/Construction Materials	4.9	7.5

Source: Central Bank of Barbados

TABLE 2

WORLD EXPORT PRICE INDICES, 1963 AND 1968-1973

	Food	Raw Materials	Minerals	Petroleum	Manu-factures
1963	100	100	100	100	100
1968	100	96	102	100	107
1969	104	101	104	100	110
1970	111	101	111	100	117
1971	117	105	127	118	124
1972	132	120	141	135	134
1973	194	184	181	182	156
Growth Rates	6.9	6.3	6.1	6.2	4.6

Source: International Financial Statistics

Freight rates for shipping between the U.K. and the Caribbean area rose by 7.5 per cent during the years 1968 to 1970 [1]. In the case of shipping from the

U.S.A. the increase was 15 per cent for the period 1968-1973 [2], while for the same period, the average revenue received per ton of cargo carried within the Caricom region showed an annual rate of increase of 7.6 per cent [4]. Although specific information regarding insurance rates is not readily available, it can be assumed that such rates have been moving in the same direction as freight rates since marine insurance is based on the cost and freight value of any one shipment of a commodity.

FACTORS INFLUENCING RETAIL PRICES

The greater proportion of the annual increase in the prices of goods imported into the country is directly attributable to the external factors already discussed. There are, however, some internal variables which also contribute to the increases in prices of goods and services to the final consumer. The main'factors include changes in direct and indirect taxes, distributors' margins and the high import content in locally manufactured goods offered for sale on the home market.

During the period, the incidence and impact of higher tariff rates and other indirect taxes in relation to the cost-of-living index were low. In instances where new tariffs did affect items included in the retail price index, they were items of minor weight. However, certain licences and fees (direct taxes) were levied on sundry professions and other services, and as a result the costs of these services to the consumer were increased. For instance, doctors' and dentists' fees rose by 33 per cent in each case during 1970, and the costs of other medical services, like hospital charges, were doubled during the same period. Prices of other services followed suit. During the period reviewed increases in the wages of shop assistants averaged about 17 per cent and of workers in manufacturing, 15 per cent to 25 per cent. Wages to mechanics and general workers increased by 63 per cent and 54 per cent respectively between 1968 and 1970, and again by 40 per cent in both cases by 1973. Tailoring charges rose 58 per cent while the prices of hairdressing and haircuts more than doubled between 1968 and 1973. Bus fares also showed significant increases during the last two years of the period reviewed.

Upward movements in levies on goods and services and in wage rates are quickly reflected in distributors' decisions with regard to commodity prices, and retail prices are, to an appreciable extent, influenced by the structure of the distribution sector in the local economy. In Barbados, a small number of firms tends to exercise considerable market power in the retail sector. The oligopolistic nature of this sector suggests that the level of prices will be higher than would obtain in a highly competitive market.

In his notes on a study of the distributive system in Barbados, McClean [3] observed that a significant feature of pricing policy within the sector was the high degree of uniformity of approach among the various firms, especially with regard to the determination of an appropriate mark-up, as well as the level and range of mark-ups applied to various categories of goods. This observed uniformity is consistent with economic theory on oligopoly, which suggests that oligopolistic firms will avoid competition with respect to price and will restrict rivalry among themselves to product differentiation, quality of service etc.

Oligopolistic firms are well placed to pass on price increases to consumers in periods of inflation, and limited competition permits them to maintain relatively high profit margins until there is a considerable fall in real aggregate demand.

The largest annual percentage increase in retail prices (16.8 per cent) occurred between the years 1972 and 1973. Two factors were mainly responsible for this. The first was the hike in oil prices during 1973 which brought about rapid increases in the costs of imports. The second was the implementation of the Common External Tariff (CET) in August of the same year. The CET imposed higher import duties on a large number of consumer goods originating in countries outside the Caricom region. However, at the time only a very small proportion of these commodities was produced within the region and local demand still had to be met by imports from third countries which then carried considerably higher rates of duty.

COMPARISON OF RETAIL AND IMPORT PRICES BY COMMODITY GROUP

Growth rates for import prices by categories range from 1.0 per cent per annum in the case of medicines and cosmetics, to 12.7 per cent for transport equipment. The retail price indices for the groups 'medical and personal care' and 'transportation' rose 7.2 per cent and 7.1 per cent respectively. In both these groupings, a large proportion of the items of which they are composed is in the form of services for which wages are paid. In the case of medical and personal care, fees for professional services (which carry a weight of 20 out of 53 allocated to the group) have contributed significantly to the price increase, as well as higher import duties and distributors' mark-ups. With regard to 'transportation', increases in retail prices have been tempered by more or less stable rates for public transport. The last two years of the period reviewed saw appreciable increases in gasoline prices and in taxi fares but the effect of this was again dampened by official control of the prices of other items in the group — tyres, spark plugs and bicycles.

The food and beverages group displays a rate of increase of 8.8 per cent for retail prices while import prices increased at 5.8 per cent. Here again the difference is mainly due to the effect of endogenous factors — taxes and value added, such as haulage and mark-up margins.Locally produced food and food with high local content account for approximately 39 per cent of the total weight allotted to food in the retail price index. The prices of these products tend to increase sharply in times of scarcity.

Import prices of 'consumer durables' and 'construction materials' display relatively low rates of 4.5 per cent and 4.9 per cent respectively. The retail price trend for 'household operations and furnishings', which shows a rate of increase of 5.8 per cent is therefore within the expected price range. Housing, however, again contains the service component — wages to masons, carpenters and other workers, (24 per cent of the group weight) and increases in these tend to influence strongly the movements in the retail prices of this group.

The group 'clothing' in the retail price index compares with 'clothing and footwear' in the import price index. The difference in the rates of growth (7.4 per cent for retail prices compared with 6.6 per cent for import prices) is not large and most likely reflects both the highly competitive conditions within the clothing industry and the fact that the major proportion of clothing imports originate within the region, with prices comparable to local prices.

Trends in import prices for the group 'machinery' display a surprisingly low growth rate of 2.8 per cent , with 1969 and 1970 prices below base year levels. The increases which did take place beginning during 1971 are accounted for by periods of heavy capital formation which necessitated the importation of high priced plant and equipment. The low rate of increase in the import prices of 'machinery' − a capital good − is another factor contributing to the relatively slow increases in the retail prices of 'clothing' and 'household operations and furnishings', the main activities in which these capital goods imports were employed.

Examination of the two sets of indices as a whole and of the factors influencing each, seem to support the widely accepted hypothesis that the rapid price increases between 1968 and 1973 was a direct consequence of high import prices, which contributed probably as much as 75 per cent of the price rise for the period. However, the data also reflect some contribution by local factors − changes in the level of taxes and duties during the same period, which gave distributors the opportunity to place higher mark-ups on all commodities.

There are several other factors stemming from the severely limited natural resource base of the economy, which influence the level of retail prices within Barbados. Low food production levels (because of constraints already discussed) fail to curb high price increases. In the manufacturing sector, the great reliance on imported inputs produces a built-in bias towards high product price during periods of world-wide inflation. In addition, the shortage of skilled workers throughout a broad spectrum of occupations puts a premium on the price of certain categories of employees, especially at the managerial level.

DOMESTIC EXPORT PRICES

This high import content in local manufacture is also of major significance for domestic export prices. The raw materials for the garment industry, furniture and other manufactures are all imported. In agricultural production as well a significant proportion of inputs such as machinery, fertilizer and fungicides, are imported.

This factor serves to set a 'floor' under the cost of production in that such costs will depend, to a large extent, on trends in import prices. Moreover, during inflationary conditions the costs of two basic factors of production − labour and·capital − tend to rise in line with other prices. Labour costs rise as wages

TABLE 3

IMPORT PRICE INDEX FOR INTERMEDIATE AND CAPITAL GOODS BARBADOS 1968-1973

Year	Intermediate								Capital	
	Fuels	Chemicals	All Inter-mediate Goods	Animal Feed	Crude (a) Materials	Fertili-zers (b)	Dyeing Tanning & Colouring Materials	Textiles	Construct-ion Mater-ials (c)	Machinery
1968	100.0	100.0	100.0	100.0	100.0	100.0	100.0	100.0	100.0	100.0
1969	93.5	94.7	107.7	78.4	115.3	112.2	105.9	105.0	105.0	94.5
1970	88.3	93.9	120.0	67.6	120.8	125.4	106.3	115.6	110.4	94.1
1971	98.9	129.5	120.3	73.0	124.6	335.4	103.9	118.1	125.6	108.2
1972	113.2	131.4	124.0	64.9	125.6	175.2	134.5	135.3	127.4	106.6
1973	139.7	166.7	131.0	135.1	160.4	185.3	125.7	147.6	133.0	116.7
Growth Rate	5.8	8.9	4.6	5.1	8.2	10.8	3.9	6.8	4.9	2.8

Notes: (a) Hides & Skins, Oil Nuts, Seeds, Vegetable Fibres
       (b) Natural & Manufactured
       (c) Lumber, Cement, Paints, Structural Parts of Metal, etc.

Source: Central Bank of Barbados

respond to collective bargaining pressures and high interest rates increase the cost of capital.

Thus, the rapid increases in import and retail prices of goods and services during the period have tended to affect real domestic export earnings. Moreover, a small developing economy like Barbados is to a large extent a 'price-taker' in the international market. With prices negotiated and fixed over time, real export income tends to fall during periods of rapid price increases.

A comparison of the trends in the import prices of intermediate and capital goods with export price trends (Table 3 and 4) shows that, whereas for 'clothing'

TABLE 4

EXPORT PRICE INDICES – BARBADOS 1969-1973
(1968=100)

Commodity	YEARS						Growth Rates
	1968	1969	1970	1971	1972	1973	
Sugar	100.0	99.5	99.4	97.8	127.9	129.8	4.5
Molasses	100.0	101.4	101.7	98.7	113.6	112.9	2.1
Rum	100.0	109.7	123.4	123.7	141.4	104.7	5.1
Shrimp	100.0	101.4	103.6	115.4	131.1	143.2	6.1
Margarine & Lard	100.0	76.3	105.4	115.1	121.5	121.5	6.4
Other Food & Beverages	100.0	123.6	116.0	99.3	170.4	145.6	6.9
Chemicals	100.0	146.6	109.6	132.9	138.4	152.1	7.2
Electrical Components	100.0	99.6	167.0	274.4	–	–	28.7[*]
Clothing	100.0	106.7	121.8	133.3	131.2	121.5	3.4
Sports Equipment	100.0	110.0	118.3	122.7	212.3	221.0	14.1
Furniture	100.0	71.4	102.6	151.4	242.3	116.8	13.2
Leather Products	100.0	100.0	112.0	105.0	132.0	121.0	3.2
Other Manu- factures	100.0	73.2	47.9	43.2	59.2	51.4	–
All Other	100.0	78.4	99.8	120.6	79.4	121.2	3.2
All Com- modities	100.0	100.2	103.3	106.7	123.6	123.5	3.7

* Up to 1971

Source: Central Bank of Barbados

export prices moved just about 3.4 per cent per annum during the period, import prices for textiles averaged 6.8 per cent. Prices for the commodity 'sugar', which enjoys a protected market, nevertheless failed to move more quickly than 4.5 per cent annually, while imported inputs into its manufacture — fuels, chemicals and fertilizers — have been showing price increases of 5.8 per cent, 8.9 per cent and 10.8 per cent respectively. Growth in the export prices for 'sports equipment' and for 'furniture' however, compares favourably with import prices for inputs into these industries — crude materials, dyeing and tanning materials and structural parts of metal.

The domestic export price index also shows that for unprotected items, export prices moved in a diametrically opposite direction to import prices during 1973 — a definite worsening of the terms of trade. In a period when world commodity prices displayed phenomenal increases, export prices might have been expected to move not at the same pace, perhaps, but at least in the same direction.

TABLE 5

NET BARTER TERMS OF TRADE
BARBADOS 1968=100

Year	P_m	P_x	$T = P_x / P_m$
1968	100.0	100.0	100.0
1969	101.2	100.2	99.0
1970	115.0	103.3	89.8
1971	138.1	106.7	77.3
1972	130.5	123.6	95.7
1973	142.2	123.5	86.8

Source: Central Bank of Barbados

CONCLUSION

The foregoing discussion on price trends during the period 1968-1973 suggests that for small open economies such as Barbados, import prices have a direct influence on retail prices. Price levels in different countries are closely linked by trade in goods and services, and prices of traded goods tend to be kept in line with world prices through international competition. This increase in world commodity prices caused import prices to rise and precipitated an acceleration in domestic prices. These two movements brought about an increase in costs in both the private and the public sector which contributed in some measure to higher tax structures and to a higher price level within the economy. Retail prices continually moved upwards as producers and distributors made pricing adjustments in an effort to maintain profit margins.

With rapid increase in import and retail prices, real income from domestic exports tended to fall, particularly in the case of those commodities for which prices are fixed over time. Moreover, despite overall increases in world commodity prices, export prices of 'non-protected' lines have not displayed comparable rates of increase, and for the year 1973 indicated a definite worsening of the terms of trade.

REFERENCES

1.   Association of the West Indies Transatlantic Steamship Lines, *Records,* 1968-73.

2.   Leeward Islands, Windward Islands and Guyana Conference, *Records,* 1968-73.

3.   McClean, A.W.A., "Working Notes on a Study of the Distributive System in Barbados, *unpublished Ms.*, Department of Economics, University of the West Indies, Cave Hill, Barbados, March 1975.

4.   West Indies Shipping Corporation, *Annual Accounts* (unpublished) 1968-73.

APPENDIX I

Methodology

The Index of Import Prices: A sample of 630 import items is chosen from Sections 0 to 8 using the year 1968 as the base year, and selecting items on the basis of a cut-off point of $20,000. In the case of exports, indices for the fourteen principal export commodities are compiled. Weights are assigned to each section according to the relative importance of the section to the value of total imports/exports for the year.

The unit value of each item is obtained by dividing its total import/export value by the quantity imported/exported. These unit values are aggregated by divisions to get what can be described as the 'price' paid for each of the items selected from the division.

The index for each section is then computed according to the formula:-

$$I_p = \left[\frac{(\frac{yc}{yo} \cdot w)}{W} \right] .100$$

Where I_p = price index; y_o = unit price in base year;

y^c = unit price in current year;

w = division weight; W = section weight.

System of Weights for the Index of Import Prices

SITC Section	Category of Import	Weight
0	Food	238
I	Beverages and Tobacco	21
II	Crude materials, inedible excluding fuels	36
III	Mineral fuels and lubricants	102
IV	Animal and Vegetable Oils and Fats	10
V	Chemicals	75
VI	Manufactured Goods classified by material	194
VII	Machinery and transport equipment	216
VIII	Miscellaneous Manufactured Articles	108
Total		1000

APPENDIX II

INDEX OF IMPORT PRICES 1968-1973

BY CATEGORY OF GOODS

Year	Food and Beverages	Consumer Non-durables	Consumer Durables	Construction Materials	Transport Equipment	Clothing and Footwear	Textiles	Medicines and Cosmetics	Machinery
1968	100.0	100.0	100.0	100.0	100.0	100.0	100.0	100.0	100.0
1969	102.2	101.8	100.9	105.0	127.5	97.3	105.0	89.1	94.5
1970	108.9	125.5	113.4	110.4	142.8	106.1	115.6	80.3	94.1
1971	115.4	138.9	118.9	125.6	158.8	110.1	118.1	104.7	108.2
1972	138.6	146.0	127.0	127.4	172.3	116.4	135.3	104.7	106.6
1973	139.9	147.7	129.6	133.0	230.8	146.6	147.6	105.4	118.7
Growth Rate	5.8	6.8	4.5	4.9	12.7	6.6	6.8	1.0	2.8

Source: Central Bank of Barbados

APPENDIX III

AVERAGE RETAIL PRICE INDICES

1968 = 100

Year	All Items	Food and Beverages	Household Operations and Furnishings	Clothing	Medical Personal	Transportation	Education and Recreation	Housing
1968	100.0	100.0	100.0	100.0	100.0	100.0	100.0	100.0
1969	105.3	105.1	101.9	108.3	102.7	100.4	108.5	120.3
1970	113.5	111.8	108.1	114.9	116.8	116.0	119.2	121.8
1971	122.1	121.0	115.7	123.0	135.8	118.5	125.3	125.2
1972	136.5	141.2	121.9	134.1	140.3	131.3	126.4	129.2
1973	159.5	166.3	139.5	152.7	151.7	150.7	151.8	154.0
Growth Rate (%)	8.2	8.8	5.8	7.4	7.2	7.1	7.2	7.5

Source: Adapted from Monthly Retail Price Indices, Barbados Statistical Service.

APPENDIX IV

INDEX OF IMPORT PRICES 1968-1973

BY SECTION OF THE STANDARD INTERNATIONAL TRADE CLASSIFICATION

Year	Food	Beverages and Tobacco	Crude Materials excluding Fuels and inedible	Mineral Fuels and Lubricants etc.	Animal and Vegetable Oils and Fats	Chemicals	Manufactured Goods Classified by Materials	Machinery and Transport Equipment	Miscellaneous Manufactured Articles	All Sections
	0	1	2	3	4	5	6	7	8	
1968	100.0	100.0	100.0	100.0	100.0	100.0	100.0	100.0	100.0	100.0
1969	102.1	83.5	109.3	91.7	93.5	94.7	101.1	114.3	101.5	101.2
1970	115.4	92.3	117.7	157.9	88.3	93.9	106.4	117.9	112.8	115.0
1971	120.9	93.3	123.8	168.5	98.9	129.5	115.7	125.4	125.6	138.1
1972	129.3	104.5	122.9	185.9	113.2	131.4	129.1	139.4	136.6	130.5
1973	156.3	119.1	125.1	205.3	139.7	166.7	136.6	230.7	149.8	142.2
Growth Rate	7.7	2.9	3.8	12.7	5.8	8.9	5.4	12.6	7.0	6.0

Source:　Central Bank of Barbados

ERROL N. ALLEN

A NOTE ON INFLATION IN THE EAST CARIBBEAN CURRENCY AREA

Inflation may be defined as a tendency for the general level of prices to rise. There are various yardsticks to measure the rate of inflation. They include indexes of producers and consumers prices as well as indexes of export and import prices. This note examines the relative strengths of some of the major sources of price increases in the Eastern Caribbean Currency Area, and focuses mainly on the index of consumer prices.

RETAIL PRICE INDICES

As a measure of inflationary conditions in this area the retail price indexes are the only statistical data upon which one can draw. In most cases the indexes are based on surveys carried out in 1964 among consumers in the lower income bracket. Since then tastes and consumption patterns have changed and so has the range of goods available. Many commodities and services which will qualify for inclusion today are omitted, and so the index based on weights which are outdated would tend to falsify the rate of inflation in recent years. Antigua, however abandoned the 1964 index in January 1969 when a middle income index was introduced, and Montserrat took a similar decision in March 1974. In order to allow a crude comparison with the other islands the new indexes for Antigua and Montserrat have been recalculated to provide for the same base year for all the islands (See Tables 1 and 2).

TABLE 1
RETAIL PRICE INDICES

	April 1971	April 1972	April 1973	April 1974	April 1975
Antigua	137.3	149.2	168.1	204.6	227.8
Dominica	134.6	137.1	149.0	212.6	N.A.
Grenada	N.A.	N.A.	N.A.	N.A.	N.A.
Montserrat	160.4	163.4	179.4	212.7	270.0
St. Kitts	135.6	140.8	154.8	198.4	218.7
St. Lucia	142.0	151.9	167.9	227.6	266.0
St. Vincent	128.7	142.4	156.2	224.1	251.6

TABLE 2
RETAIL PRICE INDEX
ANNUAL RATE OF GROWTH %

	1971 (Apr. 71-Apr. 72)	1972 (Apr. 72-Apr. 73)	1973 (Apr. 73-Apr. 74)	1974 (Apr. 74-Apr. 75)
Antigua	8.7	12.7	21.7	11.3
Dominica	1.9	8.7	42.7	N.A.
Grenada	N.A.	N.A.	N.A.	N.A.
Montserrat	1.9	9.8	18.6	27.2
St. Kitts	3.8	9.9	28.2	10.2
St. Lucia	7.0	10.5	35.6	16.9
St. Vincent	10.6	9.7	43.5	12.3
Barbados	11.5	12.1	37.5	27.9
Guyana	2.9	7.1	15.6	11.3
Jamaica	5.3	15.1	27.1	18.9
Trinidad	10.7	8.9	22.0	22.0

A similar pattern of price increases was observed in all ECCA states during the last four years. Inflation assumed relatively modest proportions up to the year ended April 1973, but between April 1973 and April 1974 there was a rapid increase in all States. This rise was due partly to increased costs of production of imported consumer goods and partly to dearer freight charges occasioned by the fuel crisis. The major part of the 1973/74 cost of living increases occurred between November 1973 and April 1974. In 1974/75 however the rate of inflation slackened throughout the area with the exception of Montserrat. This may be due to the fact that Montserrat introduced a new index in April 1974 which took into account current consumption patterns while the other States were operating on indexes that were very much out of date.

It may also be observed that the other Caricom States have all been experiencing similar inflationary trends and in some case rates of price increases that are higher than those experienced in this area. For most of the ECCA states imports from the more developed Caricom countries comprise between 15 per cent and 20 per cent of total imports, hence inflation generated in those countries, some of which were pursuing expansionary policies, is easily transmitted to the area and in time becomes absorbed into the domestic inflationary process. The pursuance of such expansionary policies accords with the monetarists view as to the fundamental cause of inflation. This view holds that monetary expansion is the independent variable in the system and that money supply is not merely responding to exogenous changes in the price level in order to prevent real income from falling. In the ECCA States however, the evidence does not appear to support this thesis. Each State experienced a higher increase in the retail price index in 1973/74 than in 1972/73, yet the increase in money supply was lower in 1973/74. In four islands the money supply actually declined in that year as is shown in Table 3. It may well be that during times of high inflation, consumers reduce and change their pattern of consumption after a period during which they maintain their level of consumption at the expense of savings.

TABLE 3

COMPARISON BETWEEN INCREASES IN MONEY SUPPLY AND INCREASES IN RETAIL PRICE INDEX

	1972		1973		1974	
	% Increase in Retail Price Index	% Increase in Money Supply	% Increase in Retail Price Index	% Increase in Money Supply	% Increase in Retail Price Index	% Increase in Money Supply
Antigua	12.7	+ 8	21.7	+ 9	11.3	+ 24
Dominica	8.7	+ 12	42.7	- 6	NA	+ 7
Grenada	NA	+ 19	NA	- 1	NA	+ 18
Montserrat	9.8	+ 39	18.6	+ 13	27.2	- 7
St. Kitts	9.9	+ 11	28.2	- 8	10.2	+ 30
St. Lucia	10.5	+ 19	35.6	+ 14	16.9	+ 14
St. Vincent	9.7	+ 14	43.5	- 3	12.3	+ 5
E.C.C.A.	-	+ 13	-	+ 16	—	+ 17

Notes:　1972 covers the period April 1972 to April 1973; 1973 covers the period April 1973 to April 1974; 1974 covers the period April 1974 to April 1975.

COST PUSH INFLATION

An inflationary situation may have social and political origins, i.e., a struggle for a redistribution of the national income. Thus persistent bidding up of wages by one group and the reluctance or inability of other groups to accept a smaller share leads to a rise in prices.

If W is taken as the wage bill and P the profit bill then in a very simplified model money income - Y - is shared out between wage earners and profit earners i.e. $Y = W + P$. A condition for zero inflation is that the following relationship should hold *ex ante* $Y_t = (X_1 + X_2) Y_t$ where X_1 and X_2 are the shares of wages and profits in the national income. Clearly $X_1 + X_2 = 1$ *ex post*. The important factor is that each income group should be satisfied with the distribution of the national income. If the wage earners group is dissatisfied with its share and if it has the means to try to increase it, then unless the other group is prepared and able to accept a lower stake in the national income the desired shares will exceed unity i.e. $X_1 + X_2 > 1$.

This in essence is the cost push hypothesis but it may be disaggregated somewhat to take into account group rivalry — rivalry between unions — where workers in one union vie with workers in other unions to establish or maintain wage differentials.

How does this hypothesis fit the experience in the ECCA. It seems clear that certain conditions must exist in the region's industries if the hypothesis is to be proved right. The workers in industry should be engaged in activity in which the employee is easily distinguishable from the employer. The unions which should act independently of and not in collusion with the employer must control the majority of workers in the industry. In the ECCA States some of the dominant unions have a close affiliation with the ruling party and if the Government or an agency of the Government happens to be the employer in the State's major industries, the militancy of unions is likely to be tempered. In such circumstances the hypothesis may not work.

In the banana industry where the fruit is cultivated to a great extent by peasant farmers on small holdings, much of the labour is provided by the family unit. Union presence tends therefore to be concentrated in the services (purchasing, transportation etc.) provided by the banana association, and even here it may be difficult to exert pressure for wage increases when it is known that profitability in the industry is a function of external factors which have a direct bearing on the price paid by importers.

In the Government sector, wage increases tend to follow a regular pattern in which salary revisions take place every three, four or sometimes five years. In St. Kitts it was the Government that granted increases to civil servants and sugar workers in the early part of 1975; the pressure did not come ostensibly from the organized unions. Even where there is pressure from organized labour 'the greater share of profit' argument is seldom relevant in such cases. All in all the activities which lend themselves to this type of cost push hypothesis which is seen at work in some developed countries, are not much in evidence in the ECCA States. In fact wages tend to lag behind price increases and do not appear to be paramount in fuelling the inflationary spiral.

IMPORTED INFLATION

In the past, it has frequently been advanced that a good deal of the region's inflation is imported; and it is not difficult to see why this claim has gained increased support. The economies of the ECCA territories are open and there is a high ratio of external trade to gross national product. Such countries with open economies are very susceptible to price increases that are not of their own making. A large proportion of consumer goods would usually be imported, consequently inflation generated by factors existing in the exporting countries is easily transmitted to the area. These territories do of course generate their own inflation but it is conceivable that imported inflation may constitute a higher proportion of price increases than that which is due to domestic forces.

In an effort to establish the extent to which inflation in this area is imported, a crude index of import prices has been constructed by using import data from two islands, Montserrat and St. Kitts. From the list of items which comprise the retail price index, items were identified as imports by referring to the Annual Overseas Trade Reports to see whether they were listed. Three years data (1972, 1973 and 1974) were taken and a 'weighted relative import price index' computed for each year. By taking the average value of an imported item (value divided by quantity) as representative of its price, and attributing to that item the same weight given to it in the retail price index, the import price index for the selection of items chosen is derived by applying the formula shown in the Appendix.

The items which lent themselves readily to this exercise were (a) Food and Non-Alcoholic Beverages and (b) Alcohol and Tobacco. Many import items which appear in the retail price index could not be included in this exercise because they were not classified in sufficient detail in the trade journals.

In the study for Montserrat a total of 30 items were investigated. The computed import price for these two categories rose by 22 per cent during 1973 and by 34 per cent in 1974. This compares with an increase of 18.5 per cent and 25.2 per cent respectively in the retail price index for those two categories, while the all item index rose by 9.8 per cent in 1973 and 24.7 per cent in 1974. In the case of St. Kitts where 40 items were investigated the computed import price index rose during the two years by 18 per cent and 22 per cent respectively while the retail price index for the same categories rose by 5.7 per cent and 17.8 per cent respectively. The all item index went up by 12.1 per cent in 1973 and 30.8 per cent in 1974.

The results of this study show that for the two categories investigated the percentage increase in the retail price index was smaller than the percentage increase in the import price index in both 1973 and 1974. This would seem to suggest that price increases in imported items had a significant bearing on the retail price index. Many imported items entering the consumer price index in the ECCA territories and which could not be covered in this study appeared to show even larger percentage increases. They included building material and manufactured (household) items. Had it been possible to include those items in the study.the overall effect may have been more conclusive.

CONCLUSIONS

In reviewing the inflationary trends in the area the evidence suggests that unions have not been a dominant force in pushing up wages to such an extent as to create cost push inflation. As a monetary phenomenon there is little to support the thesis that monetary expansion has been the independent variable in the inflationary process. The demand pull thesis was not discussed in detail since it did not appear to have contributed significantly to price increases. Output in the major agricultural industries — sugar and bananas — never reached the level attained in 1969/70 due to unfavourable prices and drought. In many instances export earnings declined and conditions generally remained somewhat depressed. However for the period reviewed (up to April 1975) most of the evidence points to imported inflation as the single most important factor in domestic inflation. This is further reinforced by the significant depreciation of sterling that has taken place since then and which has contributed so markedly to price increases in recent months.

APPENDIX

COMPUTATION OF IMPORT PRICE INDEX

I.   **MONTSERRAT**

Year	Total Weights of Selected Items	Average Value x Weight of Items	Index
1972	285	40,260	$40,260 \div 285 = 141.3$
1973	285	48,935	$48,935 \div 285 = 171.7$
1974	285	65,742	$65,742 \div 285 = 230.7$

$$\frac{\Sigma \frac{(P_{1i})}{(P_{oi})} \, vi}{\Sigma \, vi}$$

i.e. 1973 increase over 1972 $= \dfrac{171.70}{141.26} = \; +22\%$

$$\frac{\Sigma \frac{(P_{2i})}{(P_{1i})} \, vi}{\Sigma vi}$$

i.e. 1974 increase over 1973 $= \dfrac{230.67}{171.70} = \; +34\%$

Where P = Price
v = Weight

II.   **ST. KITTS**

Year	Total Weights of Selected Items	Average Value x Weight of Items	Index
1972	456.50	81,822	$81,822 \div 456.50 = 179.0$
1973	456.50	96,122	$96,122 \div 456.50 = 211.0$
1974	456.50	119,567	$119,567 \div 456.50 = 262.0$

$$\frac{\Sigma \frac{(P_{1i})}{(P_{oi})} \, vi}{\Sigma vi}$$

i.e. 1973 increase over 1972 $= \dfrac{211}{179} = \; +18\%$

$$\frac{\Sigma \frac{(P_{2i})}{(P_{1i})} \, vi}{\Sigma vi}$$

i.e. 1974 increase over 1973 $= \dfrac{262}{211} = \; +24\%$

Where P = Price
v = Weight

III. APPENDIX (CONTD.)

COMPARATIVE INCREASE IN INDICES

	1973			1974		
	Import Price Index for Food & Alcoholic Beverages	Retail Price Index for Food & Alcoholic Beverages	All Items Retail Price Index	Import Price Index for Food & Alcoholic Beverages	Retail Price Index for Food & Alcoholic Beverages	All Items Retail Price Index
Montserrat	22%	18.5%	18.6%	34%	25.2%	27.2%
St. Kitts	18%	5.7%	12.1%	24%	17.8%	30.8%

JACK D. GUENTHER

THE ROLE OF INDEXING IN BRAZIL'S ECONOMIC POLICIES[1]

During the past seven years, the annual rate of inflation in Brazil has averaged over 20 per cent, but this has not impeded economic growth in real terms of about 10 per cent a year. This success in 'living with inflation' frequently has been attributed — in part, at least — to a system of indexing or 'monetary correction' which provided for wages, financial instruments, taxes, the exchange rate, and other economic variables to increase *pari passu* with the general level of prices, thereby minimizing the distortions usually associated with inflation. Unfortunately, good descriptions of Brazil's system of indexing are available only in Portuguese, and most of the recent characterizations of the system in foreign publications have oversimplified its operation and often have been misleading.[2]

The following description of the Brazilian system emphasizes that indexing is not as extensive as is sometimes suggested and that almost nothing is indexed through a simple 100 per cent link to prices. In the case of wages, for example, prices are only one element in the wage formula, and the formula itself has undergone revision during the past decade to keep it in line with the Government's general wage policy, resulting in wage adjustments quite different from those which would have been produced by the use of a simple escalator clause. In the case of financial instruments, only about one-fifth of the obligations of the Brazilian Treasury and financial system outstanding at the end of 1973 was indexed — mainly Government Bonds and mortgage paper — and the procedure for indexing these financial obligations also has been changed several times when the results of the indexing were inconsistent with the interest rate and other policies being pursued by the Government. Finally, in the areas of the exchange rate and charges for public sector services, there is no formal system of indexing; these important prices are adjusted frequently, but at the discretion of the economic team after taking into account not only movements in prices but other relevant factors as well.

THE ORIGINS OF INDEXING: THE 1964 FINANCIAL REFORM

The general outline of the economic and financial crisis existing in Brazil prior to the March 1964 revolution is well known. Price increases, which had averaged around 20 per cent a year during the 1950s, began to accelerate rapidly after 1959. Strong trade unions, such as those representing the port workers and bank employees, negotiated successively larger wage adjustments, credit was granted liberally to accommodate the higher costs, and the resulting wage-price spiral pushed inflation to over 80 per cent in 1963. As inflation increased and the Government tried to suppress it, the distortions in relative prices also became more severe. Exports stagnated because of delays in adjusting the exchange rate; apartments were left empty as rent adjustments lagged; and electricity, telephone, and other public services deteriorated as the charges for these services were kept artificially low. Interest rates, although nominally high, were negative in real terms, and savers sought protection in real estate or the transfer of their funds abroad. Productive investment fell, as the medium-term capital market was almost nonexistent and the generation of internal investment funds was hindered by corporate income taxes ill-adapted to high inflation. Finally, Brazil's public finances were seriously weakened, because all charges for public sector services and some of the minor taxes were specific rather than *ad valorem*; in addition, taxpayers delayed payments to take advantage of the loss in purchasing power of the cruzeiro.

Faced with this combination of high inflation and serious distortions in relative prices, the new Brazilian Government which took power in April 1964 adopted a medium-term plan to: (1) eliminate inflation gradually over a period of four or five years; and (2) minimize inflationary distortions during the transition period. While the reduction of inflation has been slower than expected, the programme to minimize the distortions from inflation, through indexing and discretionary action has been generally successful: real interest rates have been positive: the exchange rate has been adjusted regularly to compensate for increases in domestic costs relative to those abroad; and rents, tax revenue, charges for public services, and other key economic variables all have roughly kept pace with inflation. Saving and investment in the economy have been high, the balance of payments has been strong and output has risen at an unprecedented rate.

THE SYSTEM OF INDEXING

Monetary correction of financial instruments

Readjustable Treasury Bonds

In 1964 the Brazilian Government issued a series of Readjustable Treasury Bonds which were indexed for inflation in addition to paying a small nominal interest rate; these Treasury Bonds have set the pattern for most other forms of 'monetary correction' of financial assets — although, as mentioned above, the indexing of financial assets has not spread very widely in the private sector. The law does not prescribe what price index will serve for adjusting Treasury Bonds, but in practice the wholesale price index has been used. The initial reception to the Treasury Bonds was not very enthusiastic, as most Brazilian savers preferred to continue converting their idle funds into foreign exchange. To meet this problem, the Government offered a new series of Bonds in May 1965 which gave purchasers an option of monetary correction based either on the wholesale price index or on the exchange rate with respect to the U.S. dollar, whichever was more favourable. This option could be chosen *ex post*, but since 1968 the rate of depreciation of the cruzeiro in relation to the U.S. dollar has been consistently less than the rate of increase in wholesale prices, and monetary correction based on wholesale prices always has been the more favourable option.

The exact procedure used to adjust Treasury Bonds is worth describing because it reveals some of the issues involved in a system of indexing. Simply stated, a one-year Bond bought in February 1971 and redeemed in February 1972 received a small nominal interest rate plus an adjustment for the intervening increase in wholesale prices. The link to prices, however, involved an average lag of five months because of delays in the availability of statistics. The index number used to adjust a Bond in February 1972, for example, would in practice be calculated and announced in December 1971, at which time the latest available price data were for October. Moreover, in order to reduce monthly fluctuations in the value of the Bonds, the Government used three-month averages of prices. Consequently, a one-year Bond redeemed in February 1972 was adjusted for the increase in wholesale prices between the periods August-September-October 1970 and August-September-October 1971. This lag can be seen in Figure 1, for example, which shows a downturn in wholesale prices in late 1966, followed about five months later by a corresponding decline in the rate of adjustment of Treasury Bonds.

The above method of calculating monetary correction on Readjustable Treasury Bonds was abandoned in the period December 1972-March 1974, and a new system was adopted which represented a departure from pure indexing. The change was made in 1972 because the system of lagged-indexing was complicating the Government's efforts to reduce inflation; as can be seen in Figure 1, inflation declined to an annual rate of about 15 per cent in mid-1972, but the adjustment on the Bonds remained around 20 per cent for several months because of the link to price developments five months earlier. In December 1972 the Government decided to eliminate this lag by using 'projected' inflation for the recent months where price statistics were lacking. Under the new system a Bond redeemed in February 1974, for example, used actual price increases to November 1973 and 'projected' increases for the remaining three months up to January. As explained below in the discussion on wages, the Government's projected inflation generally has been less than actual inflation, and the monetary correction of Treasury Bonds became much smaller under the revised method of calculation. For this reason the adjustment of the Treasury Bonds was less than actual inflation during most of 1973 — as can be seen in Figure 1. In the 12 months ended in December 1973, the correction on Treasury Bonds was only 12.8 per cent compared with 21.5 per cent in the 12 months ended in July 1972 — even though the actual increase in wholesale prices was about 16 per cent in each of the two periods.

In the late 1960s and early 1970s, sales of these indexed Treasury Bonds to the Brazilian private sector were relatively small, and their role in Brazil's capital market remains quite limited. This is because, despite the indexing feature, the total return on the Bonds has generally been below other interest rates in Brazil, as explained more fully below. A total of Cr$21 billion of the Bonds was out-

FIGURE 1   BRAZIL WHOLESALE PRICES AND MONETARY CORRECTION
OF TREASURY BONDS

(In percentage change over previous 12 months)

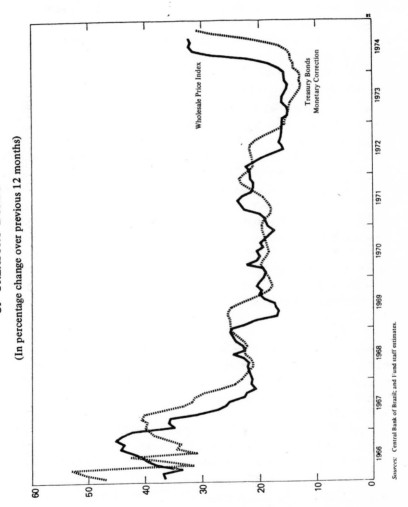

Sources: Central Bank of Brazil; and Fund staff estimates.

standing at the end of 1973, but of this amount only about Cr$3 billion (equivalent to less than 1 per cent of GDP) was held by the general public. About Cr$10 billion, or almost one half of the Treasury Bonds outstanding, was held by commercial banks to fulfill reserve requirements. This is part of a government programme to aid the banking-system — which became overextended during the period of inflation and is gradually being reformed and consolidated under the supervision of the Central Bank — by permitting banks to earn interest on a portion of their required reserves. Another Cr$5 billion of the Bonds was held by the National Housing Bank, which is the one major segment of the financial system accepting deposits with monetary correction and therefore also requiring assets in this form; and about Cr$3 billion was in the portfolios of a wide variety of public sector entities and insurance companies.

During the past two years, the Treasury has moved somewhat away from indexing, by issuing nonindexed Treasury Bills instead of indexed Bonds. These Bills were first introduced in 1970, and large quantities were sold to the public in 1972 and 1973 to absorb the excess liquidity produced by inflows of capital from the Euro-currency market. The Bills have an average maturity of less than six months and are not indexed on the grounds that the linking of such a short-term asset to a price index would not be feasible. The Bills are simply sold at weekly auctions at discounts, following the procedure used in many other countries. The yield on the Bills is, however, almost as high as the total return (including monetary correction) on Readjustable Bonds, and they have the advantage of greater liquidity. By the end of 1973, the total Bills in circulation were almost as large as the indexed Bonds, and unlike the Bonds they were mainly in the hands of voluntary purchasers.

Housing Finance

Apart from Treasury Bonds the only other major financial instruments which have been subject to indexing in Brazil are those pertaining to housing finance. Since 1964 both assets and liabilities in the housing sector have been linked to either a price or wage index and adjusted monthly, quarterly, or annually, in accordance with movements in the index. There have been frequent changes in the system of indexing, however, and, as in the case of Treasury Bonds, the Government has enjoyed wide freedom to change the index in order to meet the needs of its housing policy or its overall economic policy.

Until 1969 the principal index applied in housing was the one calculated for Readjustable Treasury Bonds, described above. The balance due on all mortgages was adjusted upward periodically in accordance with this index. Under some of the mortgage plans, the monthly payments of interest and amortization also were increased in line with this index, but under other schemes the monthly payments were adjsuted in accordance with the minimum wage — with a corresponding change in the maturity to compensate for the differing adjustments of monthly payments and principal. Beginning in 1969, however, a new system was introduced under which the principal, interest, and amortization all were adjusted upward once a year in accordance with changes in the minimum wage.

In 1973 the system again was modified, when the Housing System reverted to using for all purposes the index calculated for Treasury Bonds.

Unlike the principal and monthly payments on mortgages, the savings instruments which are used to finance housing have been adjusted in accordance with the Treasury Bonds index throughout the past decade. These instruments include savings deposits (some of which are made by potential mortgage customers), mortgage bonds sold to the general public, and obligations of the national Unemployment Insurance Fund. This Unemployment Fund was established in 1966, with all employers paying an amount equivalent to 8 per cent of their wage bill; workers' equity in the Fund is indexed in accordance with the Readjustable Treasury Bonds, and the assets of the Fund are placed mainly at the disposal of the National Housing System. The Housing Bank operating with liabilities which are all indexed, prefers to have its assets indexed in the same way; its excess funds, therefore, are invested in Readjustable Treasury Bonds, as mentioned in the preceding section.

As a result of the system of indexing, the Brazilian mortgage market, which was almost nonexistent in 1963, has grown substantially in the past decade. The programme of indexed mortgages has had a series of problems, however, including at various times a high level of defaults. The most frequent explanation for these defaults was that the family incomes of some mortgages did not grow *pari passu* with the mortgage obligations. This explanation undoubtedly was incomplete, but the problem became so severe that a revision in the system was made in 1972 to provide for mortgage payments which will decline in real terms over time. This was not done by abandoning indexing. All obligations continue to be indexed, but the initial service schedule on mortgages, which previously involved equal total payments (amortization plus interest) over the life of the contract, has been switched to one of equal amortization payments. All payments remain indexed, as before, but since the real interest payments become gradually smaller as the loan is paid off, the total monthly payments decline in real terms despite the indexing.

Other Financial Assets

Contrary to popular belief, indexing of private sector financial instruments other than those related to housing finance remains rather limited in Brazil. At the end of 1973, of the total financial instruments of Cr$218 billion issued by the Brazilian Treasury and the Brazilian financial system, about Cr$42 billion, or 19 per cent, was indexed (Table 1). The Brazilian Treasury was the debtor on Cr$21 billion, or half, of the indexed paper. On several occasions during the past decade, the Government has tried to encourage the spread of indexing into the private sector, but the movement appears to have been resisted by borrowers. Financial institutions are not prepared to accept indexed deposits unless they can find borrowers willing to assume an obligation with indexing. Private firms, however, have been reluctant to assume such 'open ended' obligations, where the nominal interest rate might turn out to exceed greatly their projections.

They appear to prefer the certainty of rates fixed in nominal terms, even if these rates are high, rather than rates fixed in real terms. Interestingly, at one point in 1966 the Government's reason for wanting to extend indexing to the private sector was because it believed that this would lead to a reduction in interest rates. At that time inflation had declined, but inflationary expectations remained strong and nominal interest rates remained high. The Government, convinced of the effectiveness of its own anti-inflationary programme, believed that interest rates of 5-10 per cent plus monetary correction would produce lower rates than those prevailing in the market. Thus, between March and May 1966 the Government even issued a special series of one-year Readjustable Treasury Bonds with the proceeds designed for re-lending to the private sector. The Treasury agreed to pay 6 per cent interest plus monetary correction on the Bonds and re-lent the funds to the private sector at a flat 24 per cent. Because of a large devaluation — the Bonds had an exchange rate option — the Treasury ended up paying a total of 55 per cent for the funds, and this attempt to extend indexing to the private sector was discontinued after heavy losses to the Treasury.

TABLE 1

BRAZIL: PRINCIPAL FINANCIAL INSTRUMENTS ISSUED BY THE TREASURY AND THE FINANCIAL SYSTEM
(In Billions of Cruzeiros)

	December 1973
Total	218
Nonindexed	176
Currency in circulation	17
Sight deposits	77
Time Deposits	28
Bills of exchange	37
Treasury bills	17
Indexed	42
Treasury Bonds	21
Mortgage Bonds	7
Savings Deposits	14

Source: Central Bank of Brazil

The erroneous impression that indexing is very extensive in Brazil's private sector is partly due to the *ex ante* monetary correction advertised by Brazilian commercial banks on their time deposits. This *ex ante* correction for inflation merely means that a certain projected level of inflation presumably has been allowed for in setting the total interest rate. The practice of *ex ante* monetary correction originated partly to circumvent Brazil's usury law, which limited interest to 12 per cent; the borrower would agree to pay, for example, 10 per cent interest and a further 12 per cent allowance for inflation. At certain times the portion corresponding to inflation also received a different tax treatment from the remainder of the interest – on the grounds that 'interest' which merely permitted the saver to keep pace with inflation should not be considered taxable income. But the total return paid on instruments with *ex ante* monetary correction is agreed in advance, and the instrument is not indexed in the sense that the return varies with the actual behaviour of prices.

The absence of generalized indexing of private sector financial assets does not mean that interest rates in this sector are low. Throughout the period 1969-1973, interest rates payable to savers on bills of acceptance – the most popular non-indexed instrument – have at all times exceeded the total return (monetary correction plus interest) payable on Treasury Bonds (Figure 2). Because the interest rates on nonindexed bills of exchange and time deposits were highly positive, the indexed Treasury Bonds held no special attraction for Brazilian savers – until the upsurge of inflation in 1974 and the lag in adjusting the nonindexed rates.

The recent marked increase in Brazil's inflation – from about 15 per cent in 1973 to over 30 per cent in the 12 months ended in September 1974 – has caus- ed the indexed Treasury Bonds to become more attractive than fixed interest securities for the first time in over five years. During 1973 the interest paid on a nonindexed time deposit in a Brazilian commercial bank was 21 per cent com- pared with a total return on an indexed Treasury Bond of about 17 per cent (13 per cent monetary correction and 4 per cent interest). By October 1974, however, because of the sharp rise in inflation (and the reversion to a system of pure indexing), the return on Treasury Bonds had risen to over 35 per cent, while the maximum interest rate permitted on time deposits had increased to only 27 per cent. This marked shift in interest rates in favour of Treasury Bonds caused an outflow of funds from financial institutions after mid-1974. The Brazilian authorities first tried to offset the increased attractiveness of Treasury Bonds by fiscal measures reducing the taxation of interest on nonindexed assets. Finally, however, in August 1974 the authorities announced a temporary sus- pension of the sale of Treasury Bonds.

The Wage Formula

During 1964 and 1965 the new Brazilian Government abolished strikes and collective bargaining on wages and ordered that future wage adjustments in the industrial sector be made in accordance with an official formula, which is described below. Total employment in the unionized sector, for which the wage formula was designed, was less than 2 million workers out of a work force of 30 million. This sector included, however, the strongly organized groups, and the

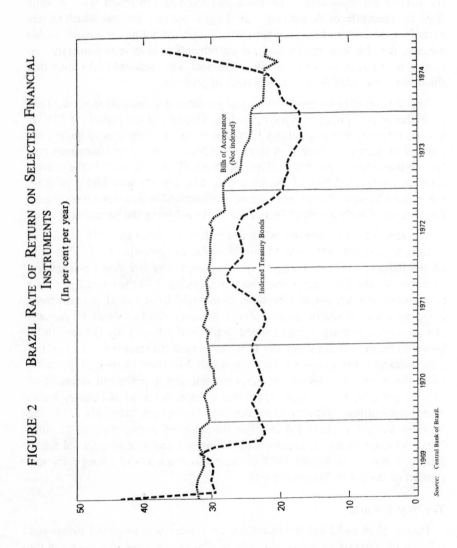

FIGURE 2   BRAZIL RATE OF RETURN ON SELECTED FINANCIAL INSTRUMENTS

(In per cent per year)

Bills of Acceptance (Not indexed)

Indexed Treasury Bonds

Source: Central Bank of Brazil.

purpose of using the standard formula for these groups was to ensure relatively uniform wage adjustments in accordance with the possibilities of the economy rather than adjustments dependent on the relative strength of each union. Other wages in the economy continued to be set by the Government independently of the formula (as in the case of the minimum wage and the wages for national and local government employees), or remained completely free of control (as in the areas of services and agriculture).

The official wage formula used in Brazil since 1965 is not at all comparable to a cost of living escalator clause operating during the life of a wage agreement. The contract is signed for a 12 month period (with contract renewals for various industries spread throughout the year); once the wage is determined there is no link to prices and no adjustment in nominal wages until the contract expires. The rise in the cost of living is taken into consideration only when a new annual contract is signed. Furthermore, even the new contract does not necessarily include full compensation for past inflation. The formula was specifically designed in fact to break the previous pattern of fully compensating for past inflation which, together with escalator clauses during the contract period, had been largely responsible for the wage-cost spiral under the previous system of collective bargaining. The formula was based on the recognition that the maintenance of average real wages did not require full compensation for the past year's inflation − provided inflation was declining. For example, if inflation was 90 per cent during 1964 and was projected at 50 per cent during 1965, a contract signed in January 1965 would only have to allow a wage increase of about 70 per cent to preserve the average real wage during the following year, assuming actual inflation was in line with the projection. Admittedly, the real wage early in 1965 would be lower than in early 1964; but this would be offset toward the end of the year by a real wage which was higher than at the end of 1964.

Specifically, wage increases granted under the 1965 formula reflected three components, which were designed to (1) raise the real wage up to the average of the previous 24 months; (2) provide for the maintenance of this average wage by granting an additional amount equal to one half of the 'projected' inflation during the year covered by the wage agreement; and (3) allow a small additional amount for higher productivity. The allowances for future inflation and productivity were announced each year by the Ministry of Planning. Not surprisingly, the estimate of future inflation always was less than the actual inflation turned out to be. For example, in the year beginning August 1966, the projected inflation used in the wage formula was only 10 per cent, whereas the actual increase in the cost of living was 30 per cent. As a result, average real wages declined during 1966 and 1967, despite the professed goal of the formula to maintain them (Table 2). This restraint on wages undoubtedly was a major reason for Brazil's success in reducing inflation rapidly in these years − from 90 per cent in 1964 to about 25 per cent in 1967 − while at the same time increasing investment and strengthening the balance of payments.

Brazil's wage formula was revised in 1968, and since that date real wages

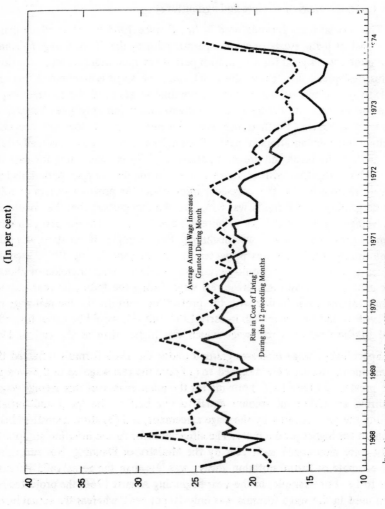

FIGURE 3. BRAZIL WAGE AND COST OF LIVING INCREASES[1]

(In per cent)

Average Annual Wage Increases
Granted During Month

Rise in Cost of Living[1]
During the 12 preceding Months

[1]Rio de Janeiro cost of living index until 1970; after 1970, national cost of living prepared
by Ministry of Labor.

granted under the formula have risen gradually (Figure 3). The major change was the introduction of a new component in the wage formula to compensate for the excess of actual inflation over projected inflation during the previous contract period: in calculating the real wage base for the coming year, the revised formula used not the real wage actually received in the past year but the intended (higher) real wage which would have been received if inflation had been as projected. Also, the allowance for the growth in productivity was raised gradual-

TABLE 2

BRAZIL: WAGES AND PRICES

	Cost of Living Used in Wage Formula 1/	Average Increase Granted in Yearly Wage Settlements Made During Month 2/	
		Private Sector	Public Sector
	Percentage increase during previous 12 months	In per cent	
December			
1966	41.9	30.0 3/	30.0 3/
1967	25.5	20.1	20.1
1968	22.8	24.5	25.1
1969	24.5	28.2	26.4
1970	22.1	22.0	22.4
1971	19.8	22.0	22.6
1972	17.9	19.4	20.0
1973	13.9	16.6	16.6
June			
1974	22.6	24.5	24.9

Sources: Getulio Vargas Foundation; and Ministry of Labour.

Notes: 1/ Refers to previous month; figures for December represent the increase in prices during the 12 months ended in November, and figure for 1974 is increase during 12 months ended in May 1974.

2/ Under the official wage formula.

3/ Staff estimate based on partial data.

ly from zero to 3-4 per cent in recent years. Because of these 1968 adjustments to the formula, real wages granted under the formula rose by an average of 2-3 per cent a year from 1968 through 1973.

Most other wages in Brazil, which are not governed by the official wage formula, appear to have followed a similar pattern since 1964, declining in real terms until 1968 and increasing since that date, In the six years, 1968-1973, when inflation averaged 20 per cent, the minimum wage was raised by an average of 24 per cent in those states with the lowest minimum and 20 per cent in areas with the highest, continuing the Government's policy of gradually reducing the regional differentials in the minimum wage. For government employees, on the other hand, general wage increases consistently have lagged behind the rise in prices, as part of the effort to reduce the number of government employees, which was regarded as excessive in the early 1960s. Exceptions have been made, however, for highly trained public servants, where unusually large fringe benefits and rapid promotions have been granted, resulting in wage increases far in excess of the average in order to retain them in the public sector. It should be added that the real wages of highly skilled employees in the private sector, most of whom are not covered by the wage formula, also appear to have risen in recent years much faster than wages under the formula.

The question frequently has been posed, particularly by those who regarded the wage formula as an escalator clause for wages, whether the existence of the formula made it more difficult for Brazil to reduce inflation. As explained above, the working of the formula undoubtedly helped to achieve the sharp reduction in inflation in the mid-1960s. Between 1968 and 1973, however, wage adjustments under the revised formula were similar to those which would have occurred under a scheme of compensation for past inflation plus a small productivity allowance. Success in reducing inflation under such a wage system depended largely on setting the productivity allowance in the wage formula below the actual increase in labour productivity. The Brazilian authorities believed that they were, in fact, underestimating productivity gains from 1968 to 1973, and they expected inflation to decline gradually for this reason. In retrospect, however, the underestimation of productivity appears to have been small, or to have been offset by other factors — including the provision that firms with exceptionally large productivity gains could give wage increases larger than dictated by the formula provided they absorbed the extra cost.

Since 1968 Brazil's revised wage formula probably has tended to perpetuate past price rises without any significant effect in either accelerating or decelerating inflation from the existing rate. There have been occasions during that period, however, when exogenous forces tended to change the rate of inflation. For example, in 1972 relatively good harvests led to a decline in the rate of price increases; and more recently the sharp increase in world prices of petroleum and other commodities together with excess domestic demand, produced an acceleration in Brazil's inflation. Once these price trends were set in motion, either increasing or decreasing the previous rate of inflation, the wage formula tended to reinforce the trend. However, the reinforcement of price trends probably was less pronounced than under the system of collective bargaining and escalator clauses which existed before the 1964 reform. This is largely because, as explained above, the Brazilian formula adjusts wages to compensate for actual price trends only when the 12 month contract expires, which means that wage payments do not fully reflect new price trends until a full year has elapsed.[3]

Other areas of indexing

Apart from wages, Treasury Bonds, and mortgages, the other principal areas where some form of indexing is used in Brazil are house rents and certain types of fiscal transactions.

During the late 1960s and early 1970s, three schemes existed for adjusting house rents, depending on when the contracts were signed: (1) contracts signed between 1964 and 1967 were adjusted each year by two thirds of the percentage increase in the minimum wage; (2) contracts signed prior to 1964 were adjusted by the full increase in the minimum wage plus an additional 10 percentage points; and (3) contracts signed after 1967 were free of controls. By 1974, however, most rents payable on pre-1964 contracts have been brought up to the market level, and almost all rent contracts are now freely negotiated. In practice, however, many of these freely negotiated contracts have clauses which link payments to the minimum wage or to Readjustable Treasury Bonds.

In the area of public finances, several types of indexing have been introduced to remove distortion created by inflation. One of the first acts of the Revolutionary Government, in July 1964, was to index unpaid taxes and related liabilities. Taxpayers had used many devices to delay paying taxes, including testing the assessments in the courts, in order to benefit from inflation while the case was under consideration. The 1964 legislation provided that all tax liabilities not paid in the calendar quarter when they became due would be subject to monetary correction.

The post-1964 tax laws also provided for the annual revaluation of fixed assets and working capital; at present, after several changes, the index for Readjustable Treasury Bonds is used for this purpose. The revaluation of the fixed assets was made mandatory while the revaluation of working capital was optional. Already in 1958 the tax laws had been revised to permit regular revaluation of fixed assets, but under that system a tax of 10 per cent was paid on the revaluation, and depreciation was not permitted on the basis of the higher values. The main effect of this pre-1964 revaluation, therefore, was to reduce taxes on excess profits which were related to the value of a corporation's assets. The new Government reduced and later eliminated the tax on revaluation; even more important, the law was changed to permit depreciation allowed for income tax purposes to be based on the revalued assets.

The 1964 revisions in the fiscal system also had the effect of permitting increases in charges for electricity, telephones, and other public services. Many of these services were provided under concessions which granted a stated return on investment. In the absence of effective revaluation, the value of the base for computing the return decreased progressively in real terms, and new investment in the sector dried up. As explained below, adjustments in charges for public services have increased much faster than general inflation in the past decade, and this provision for automatic revaluation of assets was only one part of the total new policy orientation in this area.

Indexation has been used also — but rather sporadically — for income tax brackets in Brazil, in order to ensure that the brackets are adjusted upward roughly in line with inflation. This policy antedates the 1964 reform, for already in 1961 the income tax brackets were defined as multiples of the minimum wage and were, therefore, adjusted automatically each time the minimum wage was changed. This link to wages proved unsatisfactory after 1964, when minimum wages for two or three years were adjusted upward by a lower percentage than the increase in prices, resulting in increased income tax burdens at all levels of real income. This result was not desired by the Government, and in November 1964 the law was modified to provide that the income tax brackets be adjusted in accordance with movements in prices (whenever inflation was more than 10 per cent in one year or 15 per cent in three years) rather than the minimum wage. A subsequent law, in 1967, gave the Minister of Finance power to adjust barckets in accordance with movements in either prices or the minimum wage, at his discretion. In 1973 and 1974 moreover, the Government departed even further from indexing. In 1973, as part of the policy to improve income distribution, the upper brackets were adjusted upward by 15 per cent and the lower brackets by 26 per cent; and in 1974, the upper brackets were raised by 12 per cent and the lower ones by as much as 41 per cent. Thus, the authorities have exercised a considerable amount of discretion in adjusting the tax brackets in the past decade. Although the brackets have been adjusted upward regularly, the size of the increase has been dictated by general policy considerations rather than by rigid adherence to an index.

OTHER METHODS OF ADJUSTING FOR INFLATION

The preceding section described the system of indexing in Brazil, pointing out that its use is less extensive than sometimes suggested and that even in areas where indexing is applied, the procedures are changed frequently in accordance with the overall policy goals, thereby reducing the automaticity of the system. The present section describes the policies with respect to two other important economic variables — the exchange rate and charges for public services — where adjsutments also have been made regularly to offset the effect of rising prices, but without any rigid system of indexing.

The system of mini-devaluation

In August 1968 the cruzeiro was devalued by 13 per cent in terms of cruzeiros per U.S. dollar, and the authorities announced that in the future it would be devalued frequently by small amounts. The criteria used for adjusting the rate would be price changes in Brazil compared with those abroad, the level of international reserves, and the behaviour of exports. In practice, the rate of devaluation of the cruzeiro since 1968 has been approximately equal to the difference between inflation in Brazil and in the United States. This can be seen in Figure 4 which compares the annual rate of depreciation of the cruzeiro with the differential inflation rate in the two countries.

Prior to 1968, devaluation in Brazil has been much more sporadic and was often delayed for long periods because of political considerations. When the adjustment of the exchange rate finally occurred, the change was often as large as 20-30 per cent. Under that previous system there was a great incentive to speculate on the change, with damaging consequences for the economy. Firms hesitated to contract foreign obligations, because the economic results of investments financed by foreign borrowing would often depend mainly on the accident of whether a loan was repaid shortly before or after a devaluation rather than on the merits of the investment itself. Investments for exports were particularly risky, since there was no assurance that the exchange rate existing at any future date would make the product competitive in world markets.

Although the cruzeiro has been devalued roughly in line with price differentials in recent years, this has not been done through a formal system of indexing, as is sometimes suggested. The economic authorities have been free to devalue by somewhat more or less than indicated by price differentials if that course seems advisable in the light of overall external and internal policy consideration. In December 1971, for example, the cruzeiro was depreciated fully in line with the U.S. dollar; but in February 1973, at the time of the second U.S. dollar devaluation, the cruzeiro was appreciated by 3 per cent with respect to the U.S. dollar. The Brazilian decisions on these occasions were made after considering all the advantages and disadvantages of following the U.S. devaluation (particularly the effects on the balance of payments and domestic prices) and not by a rigidly determined link of the exchange rate to price indexes.

Any attempt to index rigidly Brazil's exchange rate would encounter formidable difficulties. First, there would be the problem of selecting which price series to use in Brazil and in other countries, particularly now that the value of the U.S. dollar is fluctuating with respect to other major currencies. Brazil's combined trade with Europe and Japan has become much larger than trade with the United States, and for many exporters the rate of the cruzeiro in terms of these other currencies is more important than the rate with the U.S. dollar. For exporters, the appropriate exchange rate to index might be the rate with respect to a trade-weighted package of currencies rather than that to the U.S. dollar alone — although many of Brazil's commodity exports have a world price which is independent of their destination. With regard to foreign borrowing, which has become highly important in Brazil's economic development, over 90 per cent is in U.S. dollars or Euro-dollars; and for these borrowers the relevant exchange rate is that for the U.S. dollar, since the cost of borrowing is the interest rate on dollar loans plus the depreciation of the cruzeiro in terms of U.S. dollars.

Although the exchange rate is not formally indexed, the authorities have

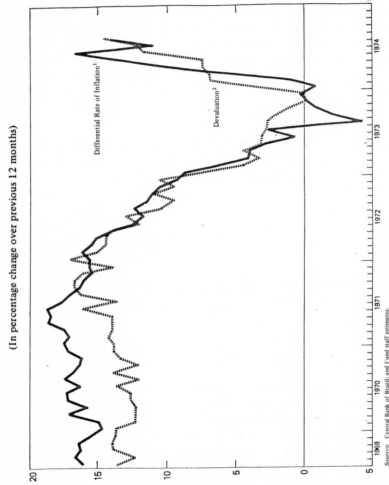

FIGURE 4   BRAZIL DEVALUATION AND DIFFERENTIAL INFLATION RATES

(In percentage change over previous 12 months)

Sources: Central Bank of Brazil; and Fund staff estimates.
[1] Difference in inflation as measured by Brazil's general price index and U.S. wholesale price index.
[2] Devaluation of cruzeiro in terms of U.S. dollars.

been able through the system of mini-devaluations at frequent, irregular intervals to convince exporters, borrowers, and foreign lenders of their firm intention to maintain a realistic exchange rate. Producers are prepared to undertake long-term investments in the export sector, with the confidence that the exchange rate will be adjusted roughly in line with relative costs and that export prospects will continue to be attractive when the investment is completed. This new policy toward exports, which traditionally was lacking in the Brazilian economy, undoubtedly contributed to the tripling in the U.S. dollar value of Brazil's exports between 1968 and 1973.

Charges for public sector goods and services

One of the most important achievements in Brazil since 1964 has been the strengthening of public sector finances, which had seriously deteriorated during the years of high inflation. As explained above, this improvement was aided by indexing of tax arrears in order to discourage taxpayers from purposely delaying the payment of taxes. Probably the most important innovation in improving public finances, however, has been the policy of frequently adjusting the charges for public sector goods and services — such as electricity, transportation, water, wheat, and petroleum — in line with the rise in prices.

During the late 1950s and early 1960s, the charges for goods and services supplied by government enterprises had lagged far behind inflation. As inflation accelerated in 1962 and 1963, the Government became even more reluctant to increase the tariffs of the state agencies. By 1963 the charges in real terms for train, bus, and air transportation, telephones, mail, electricity, petroleum, and wheat had fallen to a very low level by international standards, and the agencies responsible for providing these goods and services frequently had operating costs which far exceeded their receipts, and their investment programmes were at a minimum.

After 1964 the charges for all public sector services were adjusted upward sharply, not only in line with inflation but by amounts greatly exceeding current inflation. It was, in fact, the necessity for a large amount of such corrective inflation that caused the Government to opt for a gradual rather than an abrupt halting of inflation after 1964. By the early 1970s the charges for public services in Brazil were high even by international standards, and the large public sector investment programmes being carried out in electricity, transportation, steel, and other areas are being financed to a substantial extent by user charges.

It is important to point out that while these charges for public goods and services have risen roughly in line with inflation in recent years, this is not a result of any system of indexing, but rather of discretionary action. As in the case of the exchange rate and interest rates, the adjustment for inflation in this area is accomplished by administrative decision rather than by an automatic link to prices.

SUMMARY AND CONCLUSIONS

During the past seven years, Brazil has improved its public sector finances, increased private savings and investment, and achieved a strong growth in exports, at a time when inflation averaged about 20 per cent a year. This success was due largely to economic policies which kept interest rates high and made certain that the exchange rate, charges for public services, and tax revenues did not lag behind general price increases, as often occurs in a period of high inflation.

Automatic indexing has played a role, but only a secondary role, in assuring that these key economic variables in the economy kept pace with inflation. The exchange rate and charges for public sector services were adjusted entirely at the discretion of the authorities — not by indexing — although, of course, the general rate of inflation was the most important among the variables taken into consideration. A small portion of total wages in the economy had a tenuous link to prices through the wage formula, but this formula was changed in accordance with the overall policy goals of the Government; wages were not, therefore, indexed in the simple way which is sometimes suggested. In the case of financial assets, indexing occurred mainly on Readjustable Treasury Bonds, mortgagesand savings deposits related to housing finance; even in these areas, the Government changed the form of indexing when it conflicted with their overall policies. Indexing has not spread to other private sector financial assets despite some government efforts in this direction.

Because the area of pure indexing was quite limited in Brazil, many of the advantages and disadvantages usually associated with indexing were present only to a limited degree. For example, because the wage formula is substantially different from a simple escalator clause, it does not appear to have intensified inflationary trends in the economy to the extent which has been generally feared. For the same reason, however, the formula, at least as applied before 1968, did not prevent real wages from being eroded by inflation. Also, until 1974, the selective indexing of financial assets did not result in a siphoning off of funds from those areas without indexing. This was because the selective indexing of financial assets was only a subordinate part of the general policy to maintain positive real interest rates — with or without indexing.

In summary, Brazil's experience gives strong support to the view that removal of distortions caused by inflation is essential if a high rate of economic growth is to be achieved. In particular, where economic development has high priority, those economic variables which are important for encouraging saving, investment, and exports cannot be permitted to lag behind general price increases. The Brazilian case does not, however, provide evidence that widespread indexing is the most appropriate way to achieve this goal. Rather it would seem to indicate that firm discretionary action by economic managers is the main road to success, and that indexing should be selective, flexible, and subordinated to the general policy considerations.

FOOTNOTES

1. We are grateful to the IMF and the World Bank for permission to reprint this paper which appeared under the title "Indexing Versus Discretionary Action – Brazil's Fight Against Inflation" in *Finance and Development*, 12, 3 September 1975.

2. For the best description of the philosophy and practice of indexing in Brazil, see Chacel *et al.* [1] and a good summary of the Brazilian system by Kafka [2].

3. This lag produced a large decline in real wages when inflation accelerated from an annual rate of 15 per cent to over 30 per cent in 1974. To offset this, the government announced a special advance wage increase effective December 1, 1974, for all employees whose wage contracts had been signed between January 1 and June 1, 1974, and therefore had not fully reflected the acceleration of inflation which occurred in the second quarter of this year.

REFERENCES

[1] Charcel, Julian, Mario Henrique Simonson and Arnaldo Wald, *Correcao Monetario*, Rio de Janeiro, APEC, 1970.

[2] Kafka, Alexander, in Milton Friedman *et al. Essays on Inflation and Indexing*, American Enterprise Institute for Public Policy Research. Domestic Affairs Study No. 24, Washington D.C., October 1974.

NOTES ON CONTRIBUTORS

Huntley G. Manhertz is General Manager of the National Savings Commission in Jamaica.

Wallace Joefield-Napier is a Research Fellow at the Institute of Social and Economic Research, University of the West Indies (St. Augustine Campus).

Compton Bourne is Coordinator of the Regional Programme of Monetary Studies at the Institute of Social and Economic Research, University of the West Indies (Mona Campus).

Wilberne Persaud is a Junior Research Fellow at the Institute of Social and Economic Research, University of the West Indies (Mona Campus).

Owen Jefferson is Senior Lecturer in Economics at the University of the West Indies and at the time of writing was Director of the Economics and Projects Analysis Division at the Caribbean Development Bank.

Darcy Boyce is an economist at the Caribbean Development Bank in Barbados.

Wilfred Whittingham is Economic Affairs Officer at the Economic Commission for Latin America in Trinidad.

William C. Allen is Deputy Governor, Central Bank of the Bahamas.

Gloria Francis is a Research Economist at the Central Bank of Barbados.

Errol N. Allen is Director of Research at the East Caribbean Currency Authority, St. Kitts-Nevis.

Jack D. Guenther is Deputy Director, African Department, International Monetary Fund.

Unemployment Insuramce Fund of Brazil – 145
United Nations Economic Commission For Latin America (ECLA) – 102,104,106,
111.
United States of America – 84, 94, 112, 115, 119–120
Uruguay – 101, 103, 105–107, 111.

Value Added Model – 2
Venezuela – 101–105
Visible Trade – deficit, 77, 81, 84
  – distribution of, 12, 77, 78, 81

Wages – in agriculture, 92–93
  – real – 55
Wage Demands – excessive, 28
Wage Share, – increases in, 10, 22, 123, 134–135, 112, 117, 137
Whittingham, Wilfred – 99
Wickers, M.R. – 65
World Bank – 159

Yohe, W. and Karnosky, D.: 46